How to cope with my need for control

Janet Haines
Mandy Matthewson

Acknowledgements:
Steven Haines
Robyn Cartledge
Coverart designed by Freepik
(www.freepik.com)

This workbook offers suggestions on how to cope with the need to be in control. We do not guarantee that these suggested strategies will resolve all psychological symptoms. You may wish to seek alternative assistance from a mental health professional.

How to cope with my need for control
Janet Haines & Mandy Matthewson
Copyright © 2025
ISBN: 978-1-923573-12-3

About the authors

Dr Janet Haines has a PhD in Clinical Psychology and has worked as an academic and researcher for 17 years, and in private practice for 30 years helping people facing life problems.

Dr Mandy Matthewson is a Clinical Psychologist, senior academic and researcher with more than two decades of experience supporting people through life's toughest challenges.

For C and E.
Learning to let go to make things better.

Table of contents

Table of contents 5
Introduction 7
Why am I like this? 8
    Personality characteristics 8
    Difficult childhood experiences 9
    Experiences later in life 10
    Generalised anxiety/worry 11
    Strong problem-focused approach to life 11
What maintains this control effort? 13
Why doesn't controlling behaviour always work? 16
The downsides of trying to control everything 18
    It is exhausting 18
    People will withdraw 18
    It can significantly damage relationships 19
    Your anxiety will not go away 20
What can I do about it? 21
Controlling your nervous system 22
    What is my nervous system doing? 23
    Range of arousal 25
    Anxiety management strategies 27
    More exercises to help 34
The link between your emotions and your behaviour 40
Managing your anger 44
    Exit and wait strategy 44
    Controlling thoughts that trigger anger 45
Learning acceptance 49
    A change of attitude 49
    Worry control strategies 51
    A simple strategy to manage worry 53
Changing your thinking 54
    How are our thoughts affected? 54
    Core beliefs 54
    Cognitive errors 55

- Why do we think in unhelpful ways? 66
- Underlying assumptions of logical errors 68
- Understanding automatic thoughts 71
- Catching automatic thoughts 72
- Understanding and noticing logical errors 73
- Reframing your thoughts (cognitive restructuring) 75
- Making the restructured thinking habitual 79
- Targeting the assumptions 80

Recognising others' points of view 83
- What is empathy? 83
- What is the use of empathy? 83
- Learning empathy skills 83

Assertive negotiation 86
- Asking for change 86
- Negotiating for what you want 88

Some final thoughts 91
Additional readings 92

Introduction

Most people like to feel in control of what is happening to them and around them. The strength of this need to be in control can vary in severity or intensity. Some people feel the need to control absolutely everything and will attempt to do so even if trying to do so causes problems. Others like to control things to a lesser degree. The trouble is that we often try to control things that are not within our power to control, no matter how much we believe we can do so.

This workbook is for people who have found that their need to be in control has created problems for them. These problems might relate to interpersonal difficulties when frustrations give rise to arguments and resentment. The workbook can also be used to assist you if your need to be in control creates internal problems in that you are making things difficult for yourself and you fail to cope with the world not coming in line with your wishes and demands.

We will consider how this need to be in control began and the ways it might be affecting your life. We will introduce you to ways you can learn to function well without this level of control you have been trying to exert. It is not our goal to turn you into a person who has no control and does not want to have any control in their life. We are aiming to help you have a functional level of control that will allow you to manage your life in a comfortable and acceptable way.

Why am I like this?

There are numerous reasons why people feel a strong need to be in control to a greater degree than would be considered usual or normal. The reasons are not the same for everyone. Nevertheless, there are some common influences on this need to be in control.

Personality characteristics

Some people just have particular personality characteristics that make them feel a need for control. People refer to 'personality' a lot and use the term to mean a variety of things. From a psychological point of view, personality denotes the permanent characteristics and behaviour that make up an individual's particular way of dealing with life. Personality is made up of our particular traits (e.g., shy vs. outgoing), interests, drives (i.e., the ways we feel driven to do the things we do), values, the way we view ourselves, our abilities, and the ways in which we typically emotionally respond. Personality characteristics form early in life with contributions from genetic and environmental experience.

When describing 'normal' personality, we are referring to a broad range of personality traits that distinguish one person from another. That is, the combination of traits one person has can be different from those of another person but still be considered normal. To a large extent, this is due to all of these different combinations of personality traits allowing people to flexibly adapt to any changes in their environment as needed. This means that when the demands placed on you vary, you can adapt to the needs of that situation and adjust what you do as a consequence of the changed situation.

However, some people have strong preferences for particular perspectives about how the world works and how they fit into it that are based on their personality characteristics. This is the case for those people who feel a strong need to be in control. Although holding such a view can feel right, that is, 'of course, it makes sense that I am in control of things', it does mean that you are less flexible when you are faced with situations that challenge your need to be in control. It is certainly harder for you to adapt when you are placed in a situation where you have limited or no control. You are likely, then, to feel stressed.

Consider this example.

> *Throughout her life, Kathleen liked to be in charge. Her brothers and sisters used to refer to her as 'bossy', and they probably still do. As a child, Kathleen would become infuriated if others did not do as she demanded. She experienced some problems with friendships because of this tendency to want to be in control. From Kathleen's perspective, she couldn't understand why others couldn't see that what she was demanding made sense. She knew that she had the best plan and knew best about how to do things. She would feel frustrated when people would reject her ideas and do things their own way. As she got older, Kathleen realised that people sometimes objected to her demands that she take charge of things. However, understanding that people would become upset with her did not alter her view that she knew best. She believed that things would turn out much better if people just listened to her and did as she suggested.*

Difficult childhood experiences

Sometimes, difficult childhood experiences can trigger a need for people to be in control. In this situation, the need to be in control is triggered by childhood experiences that were anxiety-provoking, unstable and/or chaotic.

When a child's environment is unstable or unpredictable, that child will tend to be more anxious. The uncertainty that exists when bad or unpleasant things could happen at any time causes a child to be more vigilant with regard to their environment and what people are doing in that environment. In effect, the child in this situation will become anxious, not knowing what will happen next.

In an effort to alleviate that anxiety, the child will try to take control of things so that they become more predictable. In reality, it is not possible for a child to control all things, but the effort to do so and the fact that the child is sometimes successful means that the child will be reassured by exerting control.

Once this 'control solution' is triggered, it is hard for a child to stop feeling the need to be in charge of things. That anxious child then grows into an anxious adult who continues to try to control things around them so that they never experience the uncertainty, unpredictability and chaos they experienced as a child.

Consider this example.

> *Colleen is 65 years old and experiences lots of problems associated with her need to be in control. Things have got so bad that her adult children rarely want to see her, and she doesn't get to spend much time with her grandchildren because their parents want to protect the children from their grandmother's 'bossiness'. When Colleen was 10 years old, her mother died. She recalls that her father coped poorly with her mother's death and began to drink. By the time she was 12 years of age, Colleen was running the household. She took the money her father earned before he spent it on alcohol so that she could pay the bills. She made sure her siblings were fed and attended school. Of greatest concern to Colleen at that time was her father's safety. She worried all the time that he would do something that would cause him to hurt himself. Despite all his problems, Colleen did not want to lose her father like she had lost her mother. She recalled one time when, under the influence of alcohol, her father had climbed up onto the roof to fix the television antenna. Although he wasn't hurt, Colleen remembers being terrified. She identified that event as the time when her need to be in control of things escalated to a point where it influenced all her decision-making. Colleen was never able to shake off the need to be in control. She knew it was damaging her relationships with her children and grandchildren, but she felt she could not alter the way she did things. Although her need to be in control was making her miserable, she still thought her actions made sense and criticised others for not seeing that was the case.*

Experiences later in life

Although it is less often the case, a similar sense of needing to feel in control can develop because of experiences that occur in adulthood. The types of events that can trigger this reaction have the same sort of aspects as earlier life experiences. That is, events that make you feel uncertain and unstable or threatened can result in the development of a need to control. This might occur because of difficult relationships, problematic experiences at work or more traumatic events, such as car accidents. If you develop an expectation that things will go wrong, you may also develop a strong need to feel in control.

Consider this example.

> *Jason's young daughter was badly injured in a motor vehicle accident. Although she recovered, it was a very stressful time for Jason and his wife. In response to this event, Jason tried to take control of things at the hospital and with his daughter's doctors. He was determined that she would survive, and it seems he tried to use his sheer force of will to make that happen. His daughter's recovery was prolonged, and during that time, Jason found himself needing to be in control in other areas of his life as well as in relation to his daughter's health. He was bossier and more demanding at work. He insisted his wife do as he demanded, and he put pressure on family members who had tried to help. It was like he could not contain his need to be in control to only his daughter's recovery. It was apparent that the more anxious he felt, the more Jason tried to make the world do as he demanded.*

Generalised anxiety/worry

A need to feel in control can occur in conjunction with a generalised feeling of anxiety and a propensity to worry about things. Someone who worries tends to be sure that bad things could or will happen. In an attempt to counteract those feelings of worry and anxiety, control is exerted wherever possible.

Consider this example.

> *Anthony felt anxious most of the time. He carried his anxiety around with him. Sometimes, it was like background noise, but it could flare up and become of more immediate concern. Anthony believed his anxiety came and went without rhyme or reason. He could not put his finger on any one thing that would trigger his anxiety. It was just his constant companion. Without understanding what was triggering his anxiety, Anthony did what he felt was his only option. He tried to control everything. If everything was working well and was organised and orderly, there would be no risk of something happening to cause his anxiety, he reasoned. However, this didn't really fix the problem, so he just tried harder and harder to control things.*

Strong problem-focused approach to life

A need to exert control may also come from the way in which you cope with life problems. Exerting control tends to be associated with a strong problem-focused coping style.

A distinction can be made between problem-focused coping strategies and emotion-focused strategies and between people who use these types of strategies. Problem-focused copers deal with their problems by considering the problem situation. They tend to want to *do* something when they are confronted with a problem. They are most comfortable when there are specific things related to the problem that can be the focus of their attention.

In contrast, emotion-focused copers are the people who deal with their problems by expressing their emotional reactions to the situation. They will talk about the problem and cry when they feel the need. They see the value in looking to others to share their feelings about their problem.

Some people are strongly problem-focused copers and some people are strongly emotion-focused copers. Others fall somewhere on the continuum between the two extreme positions. You may be more problem-focused than emotion-focused but still make use of some emotion-focused strategies… or the reverse.

A strong need to be in control tends to fall at the problem-focused end of the continuum. Problem-focused copers tend to look for a solution to a problem. They come up with a plan for solving a problem and then try to enforce that plan. As a coping strategy for dealing with life problems, control seems like a good one. However, the plan for solving the problem breaks down when people do not agree to do as you demand or when you are trying to control the uncontrollable.

Consider this example.

> *Jacinta liked to view herself as a 'fix-it' sort of person. She prided herself on being a problem solver. She liked to think she could solve any problem she faced. Others appreciated her problem-solving skills. They would turn to her for advice about their own problems. But Jacinta found that her need to fix things often caused her problems. She could become intensely frustrated if things didn't work out the way she demanded, sometimes to the point of becoming distressed. Importantly, she would become very annoyed with people who did not take her advice after asking for it, and it would take her a long time to get over these feelings. Jacinta believed that if people did what they were told, the problems they faced would be resolved.*

There are lots of reasons why people feel a need to be in control. Most of these reasons are not associated with diagnosed mental health conditions, although some may be related to various conditions. However, the need to be in control presents a similar problem in all cases. That is, the world does not always work in a way that allows control to be exerted, and people do not always like being controlled. When you try to control an uncontrollable situation, you are likely to feel unhappy and frustrated. When people reject your control efforts, interpersonal conflict is likely to arise.

What maintains this control effort?

So, why do you keep trying to control things even though it can have some negative consequences? For the most part, you keep doing it because you cannot find a way not to do it or, indeed, you cannot come up with a reason for changing. However, you also may continue to do it because your attempts to control are being reinforced.

When we talk about reinforcement, we are referring to reward. You can keep up your efforts to control everything because that behaviour is rewarded. There are two ways this can happen.

Firstly, controlling behaviour can be positively reinforced or directly rewarded. The diagram below shows this pattern of reinforcement.

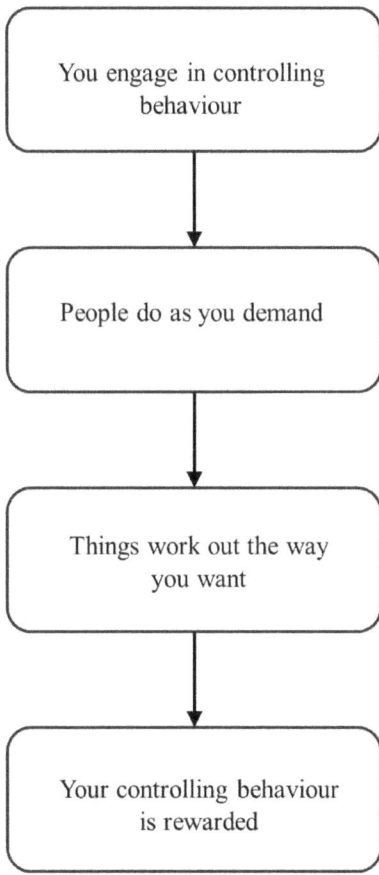

Figure 1: How controlling behaviour is positively rewarded.

This is called a pattern of positive reinforcement. That is, your action (the controlling behaviour) is directly rewarded by the fact that things work out the way you want. This good outcome for you increases the likelihood that you will choose controlling behaviour again. So, the next time you are faced with a situation that needs to be addressed, you will choose controlling behaviours again because it worked out so well last time you chose to control.

There is another pattern of reinforcement that helps maintain controlling behaviours. In this process, your anxiety is reduced the more control you exert. Consider the following diagram.

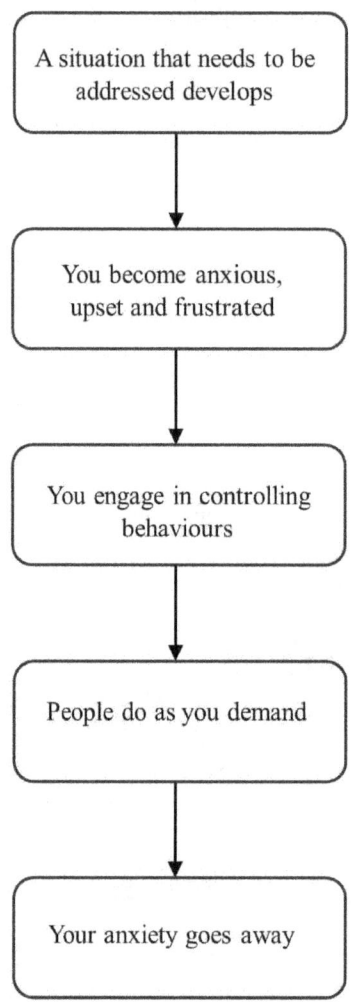

Figure 2: How controlling behaviour is negatively rewarded.

This particular pattern is called negative reinforcement. This does not mean punishment. Your controlling behaviour is still being rewarded, but, in this case, your controlling behaviour is reinforced by the termination of your anxious state with the anxious state ending because people do what you want. That cessation of an unpleasant emotional state is the thing that is reinforcing your controlling behaviour. This rewarding outcome also encourages you to choose controlling behaviours again when a difficult situation arises that needs to be addressed and you become anxious or tense.

Of course, it would be fair enough to argue that your controlling behaviour does not always lead to a good outcome, so how can it be reinforced or rewarded? Consider the following diagram.

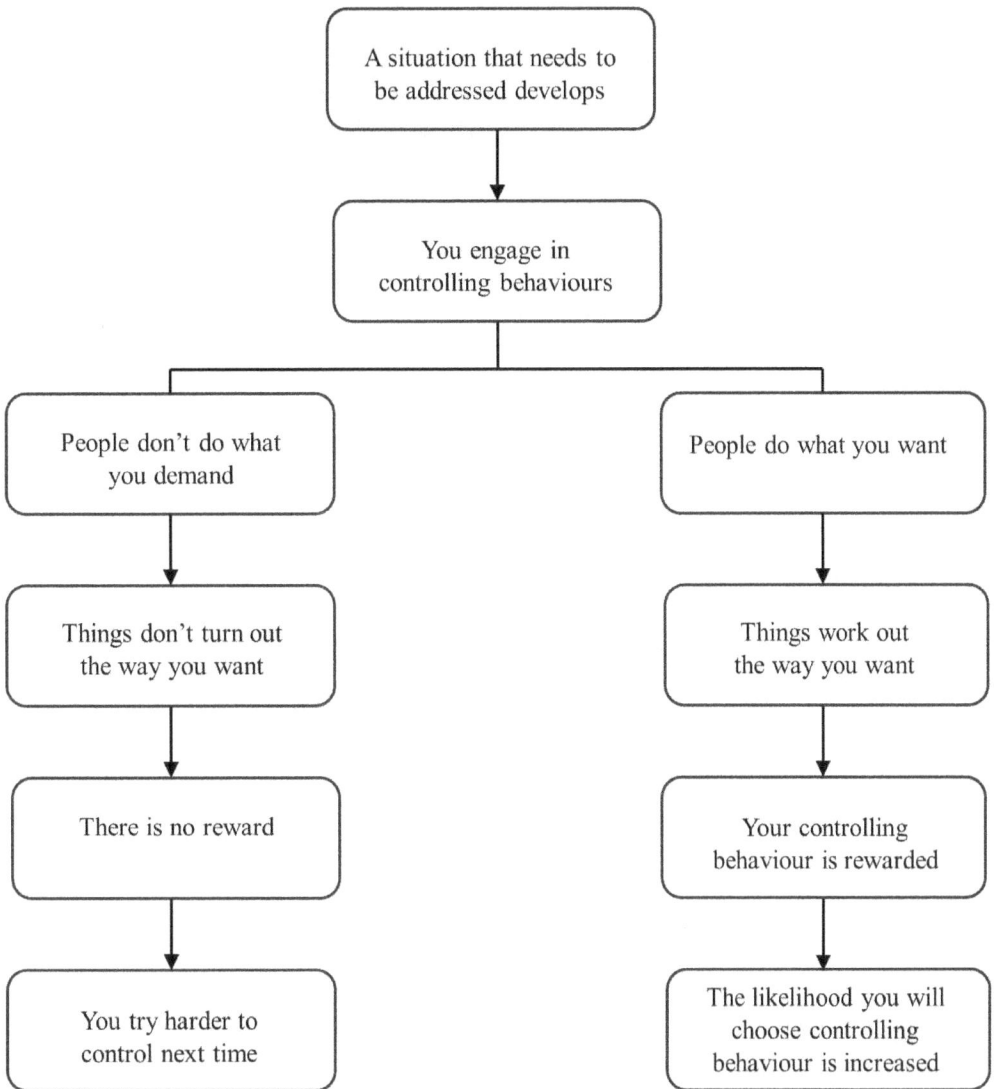

Figure 3: Why people persist in controlling behaviour.

As you can see from the diagram, an initial failure to be rewarded for controlling things does not result in you abandoning attempts to control. In fact, because your controlling behaviour sometimes works out the way you want, that intermittent reward will cause you to keep trying to control for longer than you would if it was always unsuccessful. If it never worked out the way you wanted, you would abandon the strategy and choose a different one. However, the fact that it sometimes works will cause you to keep trying and trying to get that successful outcome.

Why doesn't controlling behaviour always work?

Your efforts to control make sense to you. The controlling plan you have devised to solve a problem seems to you to be the best way to handle things. If only everyone would agree.

However, it is the case that not everyone is happy to be controlled in the way you want. They resent that degree of control and they do not like their choices being taken away from them. They may push back against your efforts to control a situation for this reason alone.

Also, other people might think their way of doing things is the correct way, even if that way is contrary to the way you would like to do things. Then, you end up with two or more people pushing for their idea to be the one that is chosen.

Consider this example.

> *Felicity had all sorts of rules she thought her husband, Ian, should follow. To Felicity, her way of doing things made sense. They meant that things ran smoothly and their lives together went well. Felicity thought her rules were flexible and reasonable. For example, Felicity thought it made financial sense for Ian to prepare his lunch at home and take it with him to work. However, knowing that he preferred to buy his lunch at a café or bakery close to work, she 'allowed' him to buy his lunch once a week. So, the evening routine was not thrown off balance. Felicity expected Ian to return home immediately after work unless he had prearranged with her, and then she would give him permission to arrive home late only if the reason for his lateness was one that she approved. There were many of these rules. Ian's attempts to bend the rule were met with a ferocity that was best avoided. This is why Ian tended to oblige... until he couldn't take it anymore. Felicity was shocked by Ian's changed behaviour. He just did what he wanted and ignored the rules she had set up for both their benefits. To make him comply, Felicity just pushed harder and demanded more.*

Of equal importance with regard to the failure of control efforts is the fact that not everything you would like to control is controllable. For a person who likes to be in control over everything, it can be incredibly frustrating to be faced with problem situations over which they have no control. Consider the following example.

> *Shane thought a colleague, Peter, should have been appointed to a position that had become vacant in their workplace. However, the position was given to someone from outside the company who had applied. Shane expressed his opinion to other colleagues, but they seemed to be disinterested in doing anything about it. So, Shane sent an email to management expressing the view that they had made a mistake and outlined his reasons for holding this view. He received a reply thanking him for his interest but informing him that a decision had been made. Frustrated, Shane emailed back, asking to be informed of the procedures available to him to challenge the decision. He received a response to the effect that he, a person not directly involved in the application process, had no means of challenging the decision, and, in any case, all relevant procedures and policies had been followed in appointing someone to the position, so it was a fair decision. Shane's frustration and annoyance increased. He again tried to rally support for his point of view from among his colleagues, who told him they were not interested and that there was nothing Shane could do in any case. Shane did not accept this. He wrote directly to the CEO, challenging the decision and, again, outlining the reasons he thought the offer of the position to the other person should be withdrawn and Peter's choice appointed in that person's place. The CEO wrote back, saying the decision was final. Shane was now angry. He couldn't understand why no one was listening to him. He tried again to convince the CEO, sending another email. In response, the CEO called Shane to a meeting in his office. In effect, the CEO informed Shane that the decision and the processes that came before the decision were none of Shane's business and that he needed to stop trying to cause trouble where none existed. The CEO said he didn't want to hear any more about the matter and that he expected Shane to work well with the new employee. Shane was astounded that the CEO and others did not appreciate his point of view. He was angry that his views had been dismissed.*

Trying to control the uncontrollable can lead to a constant state of anxiety and frustration. In an effort to obtain the reward for your controlling behaviour, that is, the outcome you want, you may find yourself increasing your efforts to control in a situation where no amount of effort will make any difference. You cannot make things happen by sheer force of will. In addition, you cannot control how people think or what they choose to do in all cases, no matter how hard you try to influence them.

The downsides of trying to control everything

We have talked about the rewards that can be obtained from trying to control things and how those rewards can influence the likelihood that you will keep trying to control things in the future. However, it is worth remembering that efforts to control things do not always work out well. There are downsides associated with trying to control everything.

It is exhausting

Trying to keep in charge of everything is tiring. There is always something to consider and something to try to control by sheer force of will. You can never relax. There will always be something new on which you will need to focus your effort. Consider this example.

> *Christine's family was having a large reunion. Family members were coming from all over the country. Everyone was planning on attending, which was something that hadn't happened for a long time. Other family members had a general plan that everyone would arrive on a particular date and then just enjoy being together. They had all made individual plans about where the people from out of town were going to stay. Christine thought this whole disorganised approach to the time together was crazy. There was no organisation or planning. People were just going to do what they wanted and just go along with whatever plans developed on the day. This was not something Christine could tolerate. She took it upon herself to get things in order. To start, she contacted everyone flying in to determine their arrival dates and times. She then arranged a spreadsheet showing who was staying where and with whom. She then worked out a plan to have various people pick up these family members from the airport, and she informed them of their duties. She then made up a list of possible activities and sent it to everyone, asking them to identify their preferences. Most people didn't respond. So, Christine went ahead and selected various activities, informing her family members that this was what everyone would be doing. And then she had to organise catering for the barbecue she organised, assigning everyone the task of bringing along a contribution. She then organised who was going to transport people to the barbecue site. She had to organise restaurant bookings, organise outings, obtain information about estimates of costs, work out transport, take account of the weather, and keep track of family members' departure times at the end of the get-together. As the time for the reunion was getting closer, Christine became exhausted. Also, she couldn't understand why the others, who just wanted a relaxed get-together, were objecting to her efforts.*

People will withdraw

Lots of people do not like to be told what to do. They do not like their views being disregarded or their choices being taken away from them. The way you feel when people disregard your wishes is similar to the way they feel when you disregard theirs. As a result, people will withdraw from you because it is too challenging to be around you. They will leave you out of decision-making, and they will be reluctant to share things with you. Consider this example.

> *For some time, Lyra had been part of a close group of friends, but she had recently become aware that they had been doing things together without inviting her to join in. Lyra was hurt and confused. She thought they all had gotten along well together, so she didn't understand why she was being excluded. She tried to reach out to a couple of her friends, but they either did not return her calls or said they were busy and would call her back when they were free. In the end, Lyra contacted the one member of the group she believed would be the person most likely to answer her questions. So, Lyra asked her what was going on. Although she tried to dodge Lyra's questions, in the end, her friend told her that the group needed a bit of a break from Lyra because of her bossy and controlling ways. She said she and the others couldn't do anything without Lyra trying to take charge and organise everyone. She said they resented this as they were all adults and could choose for themselves what they were going to do. She said everyone was tired of giving in to Lyra's demands just to avoid a confrontation. She said they all liked Lyra but didn't like the way she tried to control everything.*

It can significantly damage relationships

An overwhelming need to control can damage important relationships. Mostly, with important relationships, you aim for equality and reciprocity. That is, there should be a balance of power in the relationship with no person having more say than the other. Further, people should both put something into the relationship and get something out of that relationship. A need to exert control detracts from these important features of healthy relationships. Consider this example.

> *Ryan and Bree were married with two young children. Ryan worked, and Bree looked after the children. Bree used to laughingly call Ryan a 'control freak'. However, more recently, it did not seem so funny anymore. Bree thought Ryan's expectations were increasingly unrealistic, and she felt more and more controlled as time went on. For example, Ryan told Bree that he expected the house to be in an orderly state when he arrived home without the children's sticky fingerprints on things or toys lying around. He expected the children to be quiet. He made lists of things he expected her to achieve each day. He taught her how to fold the towels 'properly'. She had to account for every dollar she spent. Bree tried to talk with Ryan about how impossible it was to meet all his demands. He responded by saying he was only doing things the right way, and she needed to get on board with this. Bree became increasingly anxious. Things got so bad that Bree told him she would have to give consideration to whether their relationship was going to work if he didn't back off.*

Your anxiety will not go away

Nothing about exerting control will make the problem that caused this urge to control go away. At best, when you control a situation, you are creating some temporary relief from the anxiety you feel. Then, when another situation comes up, the same strong urge to control that situation so that you do not feel uncomfortable will return. It is like putting a bandaid on the problem. It temporarily covers up the problem, but it does not fix it.

We have talked with lots of people who discuss their need to be in control in terms of the 'rightness' of their behaviour. If only people could see that they are 'right' and do what you suggested, they would be better off. However, this view fails to take into account all of the downsides of trying to exert control when it is unwarranted, inappropriate and impossible.

What can I do about it?

Even if you still hold onto the hope that control is a good thing, you have probably also come to realise that trying to exert control is not really working well for you. It is reasonable, then, to ask what you can do about it. How do you change something that seems so inherently part of your character?

There are a number of ways you can go about achieving this change.

> The need to control is linked to an underlying state of anxiety. You can use control efforts to manage your anxious feelings in that when things go the way you want, you do not feel anxious. As a result, you keep trying to control things so that your anxiety state does not escalate. Learning alternative anxiety management strategies can allow you to give up the need to feel in control.

> Your control efforts can trigger angry reactions in you when those efforts do not lead to the outcomes you expect. Learning simple ways to manage your angry reactions will help you deal with the world not being exactly the way you would like it to be or others not doing as you would hope or expect.

> Learning to accept things as they are rather than constantly trying to influence things that have already occurred can help you manage a need to be in control. In this way, simple worry management strategies can help you stop the 'what if…' and 'if only…' thoughts that flood your mind.

> You can learn to identify the errors in your thinking that can underlie your need to feel in control. These errors drive you to act in ways that are controlling. By removing these errors in your thinking, you can be relieved of the need to control everything in an effort to feel all right. You can learn to focus your energy on things you can control, not things you cannot control.

> You can learn to pay more attention to the views and feelings of others as this can have an impact on your controlling behaviour. If you are more attuned to what other people are experiencing, you can take this information into account when deciding what you are going to choose to do.

> Finally, you can learn to assertively negotiate for what you want rather than demanding it. You can still argue for what you want without placing undue pressure on others to come into line with your views and without trampling over their rights by insisting that things be your way.

Controlling your nervous system

In general, people cope best when they feel that things are in their control. However, an excessive need to be in control can be related to anxiety in two ways. Firstly, anxiety can trigger the urge to take control.

> *Derek was raised by an alcohol-dependent father and a passive and timid mother. When sober, his father had been a quiet individual who seemed relatively disinterested in his children. However, when he was drunk, he would change into a violent and dangerous man who would beat his wife for imagined wrongdoings. Derek learned at a young age to monitor his father's mood and behaviour for signs he had been drinking. He would become anxious as the time for his father to return from work approached. If his father started drinking on any particular day, Derek would wait in readiness for the chaotic outburst that was likely to happen. In an effort to control his anxiety, Derek learned to control as many other things in his life as he could. To the best of his ability, he tried to make his mother safe, and he would make sure his younger siblings did not do anything to aggravate their father. By the time he was old enough to leave home, Derek's need to be in control was firmly established.*

Secondly, the urge to be in control can cause you to feel anxious.

> *Amanda felt like she was experiencing a troubling cycle of anxiety. She would try to ensure the outcome of events by exerting control over every tiny aspect of what was happening. Of course, things regularly did not turn out the way she hoped or expected. When things did not go as planned, she interpreted the situation as more chaotic than it probably was in reality, and this would make her anxious. All she could do in response to that anxiety was to try harder to control things. She knew she had to step away from trying to control things because the need for control was making her anxiety worse. However, she did not know how to do this. She felt stuck.*

So, why do you feel anxiety either as a trigger for your urge to control or in response to your control efforts? We have built-in mechanisms that react when we are placed in threatening or stressful situations. It is worth taking a moment here to explain these mechanisms because this will help you understand why you are reacting with anxiety and will help you understand the strategies you can use to help you feel better.

What is my nervous system doing?

Your autonomic nervous system (ANS) is the part of your nervous system that drives your functioning. It regulates your heart rate and temperature and makes other adjustments that are required for you to function on a moment-by-moment basis.

Your ANS is divided into two parts: the parasympathetic nervous system and the sympathetic nervous system. Your parasympathetic nervous system is the part of your ANS that should be driving you most of the time. It makes sure everything is ticking along so that your body gets what it needs and you can function well.

Your sympathetic nervous system has a specialised function. It is your self-protection system that automatically activates when you are under threat. So, if you were crossing the road and a truck came screaming around the corner, your sympathetic nervous system would activate so that you could quickly and efficiently move out of the way of the truck and reach safety. Adrenaline would release into your system, causing your hands to shake and your heart rate to increase, but you would reach the safety of the footpath on the other side of the road, and you would be fine. Your brain would then recognise that you were safe, and your sympathetic nervous system would turn off, and your parasympathetic nervous system would take over again.

Your sympathetic nervous system is attuned to your brain perceiving signs of threat. It activates when you are at risk of harm and prepares you to deal with that threat. It is an effective self-protection system when you are under threat. Unfortunately, for people who develop an overly sensitive sympathetic nervous system or for people facing challenges in life, their sympathetic nervous system will activate at the slightest indication that something is wrong and will prepare them to deal with the threat. This can occur even when there really is no threat to manage. This is what happens when you are anxious in the absence of an obvious cause of your anxiety or an obvious sign of immediate danger. In effect, your brain cannot distinguish between an external threat (e.g., a truck coming around the corner) and an internal threat (e.g., you thinking worrying or anxiety-provoking thoughts). An overly sensitive nervous system will rely on its self-defence mechanism to protect you from perceived harm.

Your nervous system will also react to crises in your life that do not present a threat of physical harm. Although it is stressful to not have things the way you want them to be, this itself is not physically threatening to you. Nevertheless, your sympathetic nervous system can be triggered by a situation where you strongly want to control things, but you are unable to do so. As stated, your brain cannot always distinguish between an external threat to your physical integrity and an internally generated reaction to a threat to your emotional well-being.

Below is a table providing an overview of the activities of the parasympathetic and sympathetic nervous systems.

Table 1: The functions of the parasympathetic and sympathetic nervous systems.

	Parasympathetic	Sympathetic
Eyes	Constricts pupils	Dilates pupils
Salivary glands	Stimulates salivation	Inhibits salivation
Heart	Slows heartbeat	Accelerates heartbeat
Lungs	Constricts bronchi	Dilates bronchi
Stomach	Stimulates digestion	Inhibits digestion
Liver	Stimulates bile release	Simulates glucose release
Kidneys		Stimulates release of adrenaline and noradrenaline*
Intestines	Stimulates peristalsis and secretion	Inhibits peristalsis and secretion
Bladder	Contracts bladder	Relaxes bladder

* Also known as epinephrine and norepinephrine

When your sympathetic nervous system is activated, a series of physical changes occur that make sense if they are in response to a threat to your physical integrity. Some of these changes are listed below.

>Adrenaline is released so that you are alert and in a heightened state, ready to deal with the threat. This causes your heart rate to increase and can cause your hands, or even your whole body, to shake.

>Your hearing and your eyesight become better than normal. Everything sounds louder than it really is, and it is difficult to tolerate lots of light and movement. This is why anxious people tend to avoid places like supermarkets. Too much noise, too much light, and too much movement can be overwhelming when you feel anxious. Anxious people tend to tolerate these things poorly because of the acuteness of their senses when their sympathetic nervous system is activated. It helps to have really good hearing and eyesight if you are being threatened, but it does not help if you are just trying to do some shopping.

In our view, the most amazing thing that happens is that your sympathetic nervous system shuts down the systems it does not need to be using. When under threat, your body needs to produce lots of glucose for energy, so it stimulates glucose production. However, other systems that are not needed are shut down. In particular, your sympathetic nervous system shuts down your gastrointestinal system (e.g., inhibits digestion and inhibits peristalsis and secretion, with peristalsis referring to the contraction of the muscles that push forward the contents of your digestive tract). This is all right if it is shut down for the period of time it takes for you to deal with a truck coming around the corner. Your body copes less well with your gastrointestinal system not functioning if the sympathetic nervous system activation is prolonged. You can lose your appetite, experience nausea, develop diarrhoea or, less commonly, constipation, and you can experience difficulty eating, or you will overeat to try to control the uncomfortable state of your digestive system.

All of these symptoms make sense if you are under threat but become a problem if the activation of your sympathetic nervous system is prolonged. Also, when your sympathetic nervous system is activated for reasons other than obvious threat, you can develop a sense of imminent danger just because your sympathetic nervous system has taken over your functioning. When your sympathetic nervous system is activated, your brain will interpret this as a sign that something is wrong. You will develop an overwhelming feeling that something terrible is about to happen, even in the absence of an identifiable sign of threat.

Later, we will introduce some straightforward ways you can bring your sympathetic nervous system under better control so your anxiety and fear are reduced. You can learn to manage the messages being received because of your need to be in control so that the message is not misinterpreted, and you can avoid that sense that something terrible is going to happen.

Range of arousal

As described, it is likely that your sympathetic nervous system has been responding to the way you are interpreting threats. When this occurs, you experience a number of physical changes that place your system into a self-protective state. You need strategies that will send a message to your nervous system that you are safe.

Before considering ways to achieve this, we need to look at one other feature of your nervous system. It is worth noting that human beings have a range of nervous system arousal within which we function the best. This range is quite large, from low in the range when we are very relaxed to high in the range when our nervous system is more 'revved up'. Pictured below is a diagram of this arousal range. The range within which you function best is known as the *window of tolerance*.

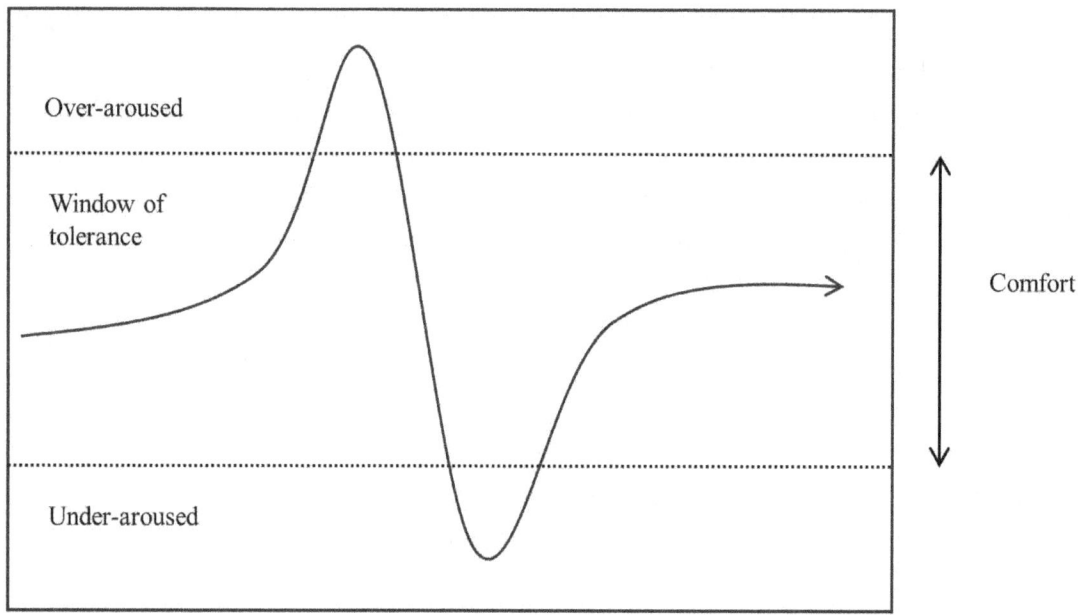

Figure 4: A diagram of the window of tolerance.

Within this window of tolerance, you have the flexibility to respond to the demands being placed on you. In this way, your arousal level will increase when you are faced with a demand and then decrease when that demand is over. As long as your arousal stays within this window, you will respond well to pressures placed on you.

If your arousal level drops below the lowest point of that range, you will enter a state of hypoarousal. In this state, you will feel slowed down and lethargic. Your functioning at this point will be inadequate, and your ability to respond to demands will be poor. If your arousal increases beyond the ceiling level, you will enter a state of hyperarousal. When this occurs, you can feel too aroused and can feel anxious and panicky. Your functioning will be impacted, and your ability to cope with pressures will deteriorate.

When you have been too stressed for a while or when you are faced with significant challenges but are still managing to cope, your arousal level creeps up from an optimal level of arousal in the middle of the window of tolerance to the upper extremes. You will find that you cannot or do not reduce that high level of arousal, even when you should be able to let go. This is why people cannot sleep well when they are under pressure. They can never relax enough for their arousal to decrease to a comfortable state. So, your 'baseline' arousal level, which is the starting point from which you respond to life demands, is high up in the range instead of midway.

In this case, your arousal level remains elevated. You barely notice this because it starts to feel normal to be under that much stress with your arousal level that high. But a problem exists. When any other thing occurs to which you have to respond, your arousal level will increase to deal with that additional demand being placed on you. However, when the starting point of your arousal level, or your baseline arousal level, is already so high, you have no room to move. Any increase in arousal will push you through the ceiling and into an uncomfortable and unpleasant hyperaroused state. You will experience anxiety as a result.

Your high starting point gives you no flexibility to respond or react to even minor additional stressors. So, the ways you normally cope with demanding situations fail because you have moved out of the range where you can successfully apply your usual coping strategies.

Anxiety management strategies

Your goal should be to get your nervous system back under control. Dealing with the challenges you face has likely pushed your arousal level to the upper limits of your window of tolerance. Extra demands, even minor ones, then cause your arousal level to move beyond the ceiling of the window of tolerance and uncomfortable and unpleasant anxiety symptoms are then experienced.

You need to aim to bring your optimal arousal level down to at least the middle of the window of tolerance, with a baseline or starting point, when you are at your most relaxed, to the lower end of that range. You need to teach your nervous system to have a better starting point and a better optimal arousal level.

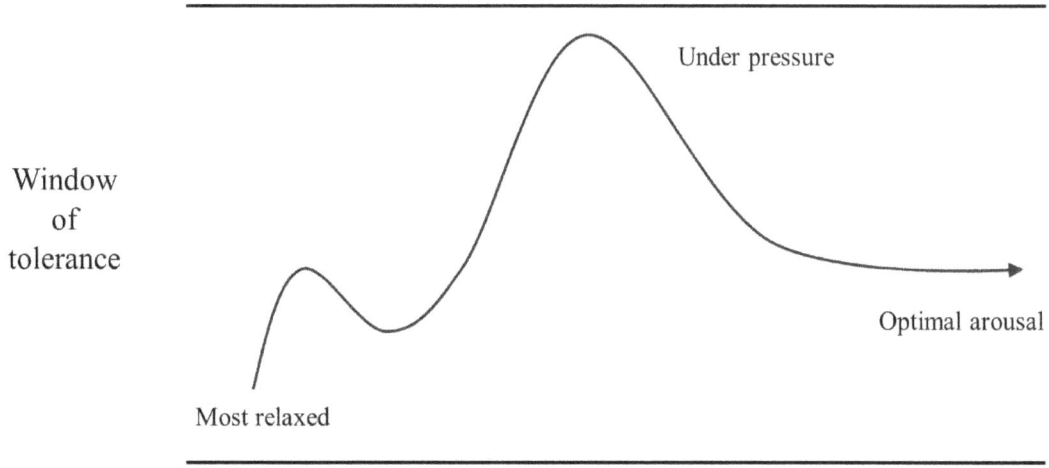

Figure 5: A diagram of an optimal level of arousal.

How do you achieve this? Consider the following. When you are in an elevated or heightened state, at the top of your window of tolerance or beyond it, your heart rate increases and your breathing changes. Your heart rate elevation is caused by a release of adrenaline that occurs when your sympathetic nervous system is triggered. This can be very uncomfortable, and it feels like there is very little you can do about it.

Your breathing changes contribute to the elevation in your heart rate. When people are stressed, their breathing tends to be rapid and shallow. You can liken this pattern of breathing to the waves on top of the water. Form a picture in your mind of the way a child draws waves. When we are stressed, we tend to breathe in sharply, then breathe out quickly and then breathe in again quickly. You tend not to breathe all the way out before you breathe in again. This inhalation-exhalation pattern is what affects your heart rate.

In contrast, when we are relaxed, our breathing tends to be deeper and slower and has a pattern than is similar to the swell in the ocean. The inhalation-exhalation pattern is a comfortable breath-in followed by a long, slower breath-out. You do not breathe in again until you have breathed all the way out.

From the diagram below, you can see the pattern of anxious, rapid and shallow breathing on the top. Below that is the pattern of slower, deeper breathing that is characteristic of a more relaxed state.

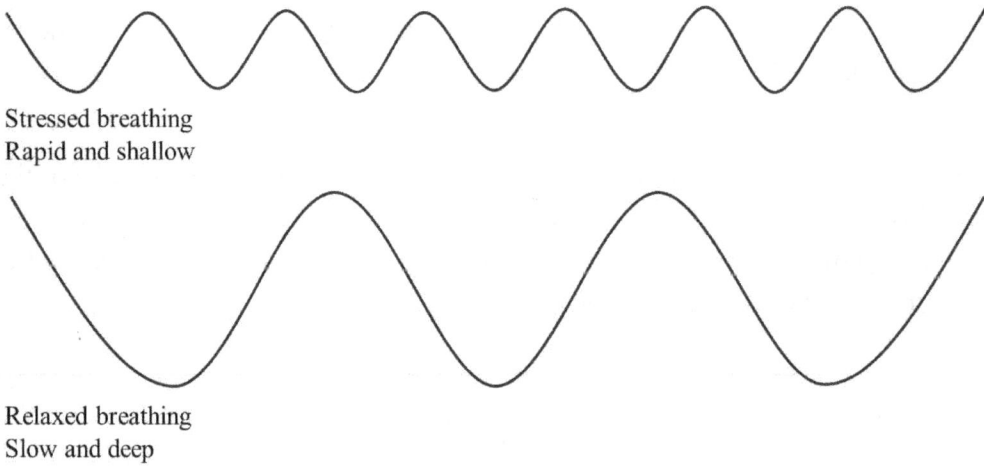

Figure 6: A comparison between stressed and relaxed breathing patterns.

The reason your breathing pattern affects your heart rate is because these two things are linked. Under normal, stress-free conditions, you heart rate increases as you breathe in and then slows as you breathe out. This is normal. When you are stressed and your respiration rate increases and your breathing is shallower, you heart rate does not have a chance to slow before you breathe in again. Therefore, you heart rate is elevated and stays that way.

Let's, for a moment, go back to the truck speeding around the corner, threatening to run you over. Your sympathetic nervous system is activated, allowing you to be in the right physical state to move quickly out of harm's way and protect yourself. When you get to the other side of the road, the truck goes past, and you are unharmed; your brain registers these experiences, your sympathetic nervous system turns off, and your parasympathetic nervous system takes over. This is because reaching the other side of the road and seeing the truck pass you by are safety signals. Your brain interprets these signs as indicators that you are going to be all right.

Of course, no such safety signals are available when you are doing too much, sitting in your loungeroom worrying, or shopping at the supermarket. They are not that sort of event. Your brain would struggle to identify safety indicators because they do not exist in that sort of form. What you can do is offer your brain a safety signal but of a different type.

You can send a message that everything is all right by deliberately slowing your heart rate from its elevated rate to a more normal rate for you. Although it sounds difficult to achieve, that is controlling your heart rate, it actually is a reasonably straightforward undertaking. If you slow your breathing and lengthen your exhalation until you have breathed all the way out before breathing back in, your heart rate will come into line, and your heart rate will go down.

To use our waves and ocean swell analogy, the aim is to change the pattern of your breathing from waves on the top of the water to a pattern like the swell in the ocean, where the water is lifted up and then put back down as the swell passes. You are aiming for an easy, comfortable breath in, followed by a long, slow breath out.

The ideal situation is to breathe out for twice as long as it takes you to breathe in. Elongating your exhalation requires that you slow the amount of air you breathe out so that you can breathe out for longer. You should aim to breathe all the way out, emptying your lungs, before you gently and comfortably breathe back in.

This pattern of breathing should result in a slowed heart rate and a subsequent reduction in that sense of anxiety or crisis that occurs when your sympathetic nervous system is triggered. This occurs because your brain interprets the reduction in heart rate and the change in breathing pattern as a signal that the crisis is over.

Let's consider a simple exercise to control your breathing by deepening your breaths and slowing them down.

	Slowing and controlling your breathing
1.	Without trying to change your breathing, just notice for a moment the pattern of your inhalations and exhalations.
2.	Now, take a comfortable breath in. It does not have to be too deep, rather just a comfortable breath.
3.	Now, breathe out, slowing the amount of air you exhale and lengthening your breath as a result.
4.	When your lungs feel empty of air, gently and comfortably breathe back in.
5.	As you breathe, practice lengthening your exhalation just a bit. You may also deepen your breath in slightly. Keep in mind the picture of the ocean swell if this helps.
6.	Practice this pattern of breathing for as long as you feel comfortable.

Exercise available at elemen.com.au

There is another element that you can add to this breathing exercise that may help with your ultimate goal of reducing your anxiety and signalling your sympathetic nervous system to turn off so your parasympathetic nervous system can do its job. You can include in this breathing exercise the element of reducing your muscle tension.

People who are stressed tend to have tense muscles. Although this muscle tension can occur anywhere in the body, common sites include the forehead and scalp, neck, jaw, shoulders, and chest. The increased muscle tension contributes to the overall sense of readiness to deal with threats. On the downside, tense muscles can cause headaches, chest and other pain.

If tense muscles present a significant problem for you, then a progressive muscle relaxation exercise may help. A general overview of this technique is provided below. More comprehensive versions are available online. However, another easy strategy is to link the relaxation of muscles with the breathing exercise.

As you breathe out, just relax your muscles in places where they feel tight and tense. You do not have to achieve marked muscle relaxation to experience a noticeable difference. Just drop your shoulders, relax your jaw, smooth your forehead or relax your stomach muscles. Aim for a gentle relaxation of tight muscles as you exhale.

The combination of breathing exercise and muscle relaxation can be used even when the focus is on controlling your breathing. You can also use the combined technique when your primary focus is on troubling muscle tension. In combination, the techniques can help with either target.

Combined breathing and muscle relaxation technique	
1.	Take a comfortable breath in. It does not have to be too deep, but rather just a comfortable breath.
2.	Now, breathe out, slowing the amount of air you exhale and lengthening your breath as a result. As you breathe out, drop your shoulders, relax your jaw, smooth your forehead and relax your abdominal muscles.
3.	When your lungs feel empty of air, gently and comfortably breathe back in.
4.	As you breathe, practice lengthening your exhalation just a bit. You may also deepen your breath in slightly. Keep in mind the picture of the ocean swell if this helps. Continue to relax your muscles slightly on each exhalation.
5.	Practice this pattern of breathing and muscle relaxation for as long as you feel comfortable.

Exercise available at elemen.com.au

As stated, if muscle tension presents you with a significant problem, you may wish to try a method of progressive muscle relaxation. This technique involves tensing your muscles and then relaxing them. Tensing your muscles before relaxing them has a number of purposes. It helps you to clearly identify where the tension in your body is located. It helps you feel the difference between a tense muscle and a relaxed one, which is helpful when the muscle has been tense for a long time. Finally, tensing the muscle first helps to induce deeper relaxation in that muscle when you relax it.

We will start with a longer version of the progressive muscle relaxation exercise that will help you learn the technique. You can then change to a shorter version that we describe below.

Progressive muscle relaxation (longer version)	
1.	Choose a comfortable place where it is quiet. Lay down or sit in a comfortable position with your feet flat on the floor.
2.	Now clench both your fists… tighter and tighter. Notice the tension in your muscles. Keep them clenched for about 10 seconds. Now relax. Feel your muscles relax. Notice the difference between the tension and relaxation.
3.	Repeat the procedure with your fists. Notice the difference between tension and relaxation.

4.	Now bend your elbows on both arms and tense your biceps. Hold the tension. Now relax. Notice the difference between tension and relaxation.
5.	Repeat the procedure with your elbows bent and your biceps tensed. Hold the tension, then relax. Pay attention to the change from tension to relaxation.
6.	Now, frown as hard as you can. Notice the tension in your forehead. Hold the tension. Now relax. Notice the difference you feel after you have released the tension.
7.	Now frown again as hard as you can. Hold the tension, then release it. Notice the contrast between tension and relaxation.
8.	Now close your eyes and squint them tightly. Hold the tension then relax. Allow your eyes to feel a comfortable relaxed state. Notice the change. Repeat by closing your eyes and squinting then relaxing, letting go of the tension.
9.	Now, clench your jaw. Bite down hard. Notice the tension throughout your jaw. Now, relax your jaw, allowing your teeth to fall apart slightly. Notice the feeling of relaxation. Repeat this exercise with your jaw.
10.	Now press your tongue hard against the roof of your mouth. Hold it there. Feel the tension at the back of your mouth. Now relax. Notice the difference between the tension and relaxation. Repeat the exercise with your tongue.
11.	Now purse your lips, pushing them out into an 'O' shape. Hold them there. Now release the tension and relax. Notice how your mouth feels now that it is relaxed. Repeat the exercise with your lips.
12.	Now press your head back as far as it will comfortably go. Hold onto the tension. Roll your head from the right to the left, allowing the focus of the tension to change. Now relax. Feel the difference between the tension in your neck and the relaxation. Repeat the exercise by pressing your head back.
13.	Now, bring your head forward with your chin on your chest. Feel the tension in your throat and the back of your neck. Hold the tension, then relax and allow your head to return to a comfortable position. Repeat the exercise by bringing your head forward.
14.	Now, shrug your shoulders, bringing your shoulders up and allowing your head to hunch down between them. Hold the tension. Now relax and notice the difference between tension and relaxation.

15.	Now breathe in deeply and hold your breathe. Hold it. Now allow yourself to gently exhale, letting go of the tension as you breathe out. Feel your body relax. Repeat the exercise, breathing in then gently letting go.
16.	Now tense your stomach muscles. Hold onto the tension. Now relax. Let your stomach muscles relax and appreciate that feeling. Repeat the exercise with your stomach muscles.
17.	Now arch your back without straining. Hold onto the tension. Now let it go. Notice the change in your muscles. Now repeat the exercise by arching your back.
18.	Now tighten your buttocks and thighs. Press down on your heels to flex your thigh muscles. Hold onto the tension. Now relax and notice the difference. Repeat the exercise.
19.	Now curl your toes downward to cause your calves to tense. Hold onto the tension. Now relax. Repeat the exercise.
20.	Now, draw your toes upward, causing your shins to feel tense. Pay attention to the tension. Now relax. Repeat the exercise.
21.	Now, scan your body. Notice if there are any tense spots. Repeat the exercise in that area.
22.	Enjoy the more relaxed feeling throughout your entire body. When you are ready, slowly return to your normal activities, holding on to that feeling of relaxation.

Exercise available at elemen.com.au

Once you have learned the technique, you can use a shorter version. You may prefer to just focus on the areas of your body that are particularly tense. It is certainly the case that some people tend to carry their muscle tension in one or two areas. Here is a shorter version that will allow you to tailor the procedure to suit your own needs.

Relaxing using progressive muscle relaxation (short version)	
1.	Choose a comfortable place where it is quiet. Lay down or sit in a comfortable position with your feet flat on the floor.
2.	Begin to work your way through groups of muscles by tensing them and relaxing them. For example, if you start with your forehead, tighten the muscles in your forehead by frowning. Hold for a few moments (10-15 seconds), then release, allowing the muscle in your forehead to relax, enjoying that experience for about 60 seconds. Notice the difference between the tension and the relaxation.
3.	Then, move on to the next group of muscles. You can work through groups of muscles from the top of your head to the tips of your toes, or you can select areas of your body that present a particular problem of tension for you.
4.	Repeat the process until you have worked your way through the groups of muscles you have selected.
5.	Repeat that process again, first tensing the muscles, holding that tension for five to ten seconds, and then relaxing those muscles.

Exercise available at elemen.com.au

So, controlling your breathing and, thus, lowering your heart rate will help you feel less anxious, as will reducing your muscle tension. However, there are other approaches you can take to anxiety management.

More exercises to help

One of the problems with being anxious and 'revved up' is that your mind fills up with anxiety-provoking thoughts. When you are trying to control your life in an excessive way, you cannot seem to stop thinking in an endless stream of anxiety-provoking thoughts. This makes it very difficult to get your nervous system back under control. The thoughts racing through your mind do not allow you to relax. So, included here are some exercises that should help you settle your mind.

The first exercises aim to teach you to self-soothe. If you can learn to settle yourself, the racing thoughts in your mind may follow. The quieter your nervous system, the less active your mind is with anxiety-provoking thoughts.

What you are aiming to do is find ways to soothe yourself. Most of us can understand how we go about soothing an upset child. We might hold and rock a distressed child and say soothing things. What you are looking for are adult versions of self-soothing strategies that will help to alleviate your distressed state.

The goal of developing self-soothing strategies is to create for yourself some moments of less distress. The strategies are aimed at reducing your heightened state to a more manageable level. They allow your nervous system arousal level to be brought back under your control. So, strategies that allow you to focus on the here and now are the ones that will allow you to choose to be in a quieter state with a greater sense of peace of mind.

Consider the proposed self-soothing strategies listed below and select ones that you think might assist you. These may be things you have tried before or ones you feel might work for you. Some of these strategies require you to make the effort to seek out the means of engaging with them. However, others are using things that are readily available or easily obtained.

	Self-soothing strategies
	Take a shower or a warm bath. Focus your attention on the sensations created by the water. Enjoy the feeling of the water on your skin and the warmth of the water.
	Play with your pet, or just stroke your dog's or cat's coat. Interacting with your pet has been demonstrated to be soothing for many pet owners.
	Change into your most comfortable clothes. Enjoy the feel of the fabric and the degree of comfort you feel from wearing these items of clothing.
	Go for a swim. Enjoy the sensation of being in the water. Allow those sensations to quiet your mind. Even if you are not a good swimmer, bobbing around in the water can produce the same sensations.
	Treat yourself to a massage if that appeals to you. Allow your muscles to relax and your mind to quiet.
	Listen to soothing music. Allow your attention to be directed to the music rather than have the music in the background.
	Listen to an audiobook, even if your distress makes it difficult to concentrate. Try to pay attention to each word that is spoken. If you lose track of the story, you can always return to the previous track and pick up the story again.
	Turn on the television or talkback radio and engage in listening to what is being broadcast. The goal here is to focus your attention on the conversations as they play out rather than selecting a programme you are excited to watch or listen to. It is the process of listening to others talking that is soothing.

	Listen to the sounds of water running. Again, the aim is to listen to the sounds of the water, stopping your mind from going to other intrusive thoughts. You can find the sound of running water in various places. You can visit a naturally occurring water course or waterfall. You could listen to running water from an outdoor garden fountain. However, you can also get an indoor personal fountain that can be used at any time. Alternatively, you can listen to recorded sounds of water running.
	Find something soothing to look at. This might be by the water or an outdoor space such as a park. It could be photographs or paintings that you find soothing or relaxing. The goal is to find something to look at that is engaging for you, and that you find relaxing and soothing.
	Spend some time outside in nature. Notice the freshness of the air. See the colours around you. Feel the breeze on your face. Notice the smell of the plants. Listen to the natural sounds around you.

Exercise available at elemen.com.au

Building on this notion of self-soothing, it is a good idea to be more present in your focus. If you give it some consideration, you will find that the thoughts racing through your mind when you are anxious typically are not related to what is happening in the here and now. Our thoughts tend to engage in time-travelling, that is, they are focused either on what has already happened or what is to come. They rarely focus on what is happening in the present moment when you are trying to relax.

Usually, at these times, nothing is happening that is worth immediately worrying about. If you could deliberately spend more time focused on the here and now and less time on the past or future, you would have a better chance of relaxing and quieting your overly stimulated nervous system.

The notion of focusing on the here and now is based on mindfulness techniques. Mindfulness refers to your ability to be aware of your emotions, your physical state, your actions and your thoughts in a state of mind that is absent from judgment or criticism of your experience. Research has demonstrated that mindfulness helps you to control symptoms of anxiety, to control the distress caused by particular situations, to increase your capacity to relax, and to learn how to cope better with challenging situations.

Based on the notion of mindfulness, we have included some exercises you can use to quiet your mind by focusing on the here and now. To do this well, you may need to practice the skill. When you first learn these techniques, it is easy to become distracted and return to your racing thoughts. Do not worry if this happens. Just return to your exercise and continue.

	Mindful listening
1.	Sit in a comfortable place, preferably by yourself. If you wish, close your eyes.
2.	Start to focus your attention on the sounds around you.
3.	Notice the changes in the sounds from moment to moment.
4.	Notice the times between sounds when it is quiet.
5.	Focus your attention both on what is happening inside and outside.
6.	Pay attention to the sounds and nothing else. Do not make judgments about the sounds. Just acknowledge the sound then listen to the next one.
7.	If thoughts about other things come into your mind, put them aside and then return to listening to the sounds around you.
8.	Do this for a few minutes or until you are ready to stop.

Exercise available at elemen.com.au

Let's try another mindfulness exercise.

	Mindful use of your senses
Sight	Look around you. Allow your attention to be drawn to five things in your immediate environment that you might not normally pay any attention to. For example, this might be the way the fruit is sitting in the fruit bowl, the way your curtain is hanging, or the way your books are placed on your bookcase. Allow your attention to rest on each of these things. Keep your focus directed at the item, setting aside any other thoughts that come into your mind.
Touch	Bring your attention to four things you can feel at this moment in time. For example, it may be the feel of the sun on your skin, or the feel of the fabric of your clothes against your skin, or the feel of the chair underneath you, or the feel of the table surface where your hand is resting. Allow your attention to rest on each of these feelings. Keep your focus directed at each sense of touch, setting aside any other thoughts that come into your mind.
Hearing	Listen to the sounds in your surroundings. Notice three things you can hear. For example, you might hear the sounds of cars travelling along the road, the noise of the refrigerator, or the sound of the wind in the trees. Focus your attention on each of these sounds. If other thoughts come into your mind, let those thoughts go and return to focusing on the sounds you can hear.
Smell	Pay attention and search for two things you can smell. For example, you might be able to smell whatever you are cooking, the scent of plants in your garden, or the sea air if you live near the water. Keep your attention focused on each of these smells. If other distracting thoughts come into your mind, let these thoughts go and return to focusing on the things you can smell.
Taste	When you are eating, focus your attention on the tastes you are experiencing. For example, take a sip of your coffee and notice the taste. Bite into your sandwich and notice the flavours. Really pay attention to the flavours of the things you are tasting. If you become distracted, let go of these interfering thoughts and return to focusing on the things you are tasting.

Exercise available at elemen.com.au

And there is one last mindfulness exercise.

	Mindful walking
1.	As you are ready to go for your walk, stand still for a moment. Sense the weight on your feet as your stand there. Feel how your muscles are supporting you and maintaining your stability and balance. Be aware of your arms in a comfortable position of your choice (e.g., by your side or hands clasped, either at the front or at your back). Allow yourself to stand there, relaxed but alert.
2.	Begin to walk. Choose a comfortable pace, not too fast and not too slow. Pay attention to how your feet and legs feel (e.g., their heaviness or lightness, energy, or even any pain). The way your legs and feet feel will form the focus of your attention. If you become distracted, return to focusing on your legs and feet.
3.	Pay attention to the way in which you lift your feet and place them back down on the surface on which you are walking. Notice how you lift your foot, swing your leg and place your foot down again ahead of where you were a moment before. Walk in a natural and relaxed manner. Move your arms in a way that feels normal for you.
4.	It is likely that your mind will wander as you walk along. Your attention will be drawn to what is around you or thoughts that come into your mind. Acknowledge that you have been distracted and return to focusing on the process of walking… the lifting of your foot, the swing of your leg and the placement of your foot in front of you. Just gently return your attention to the sensations of walking.
5.	You might focus on a point ahead of you. Focus on the steps you take as you move towards that point. One step at a time. Experience fully the sensations of walking.
6.	Keep walking mindfully until you reach your destination or the point where you decide to turn around and mindfully walk back to where you started.

Exercise available at elemen.com.au

These types of strategies can help you feel settled. However, it is not only a matter of managing your nervous system arousal if you want to feel more settled. It is also necessary to consider the link between your emotional state and the ways you choose to act.

The link between your emotions and your behaviour

When you are driven by the urge to control everything and when your control efforts do not work as you expect, you can feel strong emotions. This can be a difficult and uncomfortable time. It would be helpful for you to be able to manage those strong emotions.

This does not mean that you should fight against the emotions you feel. You cannot start a war with your emotional state and expect to be the victor. Nor can you ignore your emotions and expect them to just disappear. The aim should be to recognise and validate your emotional reactions, but do what you can to avoid your emotional distress escalating.

It is worthwhile to understand the link between your emotional state and the things you choose to do in response to that emotion. This is important. It is difficult to control your behaviour choices if you do not appreciate the link between how you feel and what you do.

Let's consider how you might behave in relation to your emotional responses. Consider this example.

Imagine you have been experiencing increasing tensions with your partner about the way he does things around the home. Despite you making it clear about how things should be done, your partner tends to do things their own way. Today, your partner cooked dinner but prepared the meal in a way different from the way you instructed him.	
I felt	What I did
Angry	*I refused to eat what he had prepared, left the room, and refused to speak to my partner.*
Anxious	*I paced around and couldn't settle down.*

Understanding this link between your emotional state and your behaviour can help you learn to make different choices in how you act when you are upset. We will explore this further when we consider building your coping strategies, but let's consider here how you might opt to do different things. Consider the same example but now let's look at how this person might have chosen to do things differently.

I felt	What I did	What I could have done instead
Angry	*I refused to eat what he had prepared, left the room, and refused to speak to my partner.*	*I could have eaten the meal my partner had prepared for me.*
Anxious	*I paced around and couldn't settle down.*	*I could have implemented an anxiety control strategy I had learned.*

Let's take this one step further and consider the likely outcomes of the initial behaviour choice and the alternative one.

I felt…	*Angry.*
I did…	*I refused to eat what he had prepared, left the room, and refused to speak to my partner.*
What happened?	*I continued to feel angry. I wouldn't back down, and my partner and I ended up sleeping in separate rooms.*
A better choice…	*I could have accepted that my partner was entitled to prepare the meal in whatever way they chose. I could have realised that my thoughts about how the meal should have been prepared should not have affected the rest of our evening and created a rift between us.*
Likely outcome…	*I would have felt better much sooner. I could have had a pleasant and relaxing evening, and things would have been normal.*
I felt…	*Anxious*
I did…	*I paced around and couldn't settle.*
What happened?	*My anxiety got worse and worse until I couldn't deal with it, so I went on to spend a restless night in the guest bedroom.*

A better choice…	*I could have recognised that my anxiety was causing me to make poor choices and implemented an anxiety management strategy. This would have allowed me to bring my anxiety under control.*
Likely outcome…	*My anxiety would have passed, and I would have been able to have a relaxing evening. We would have gone to bed as normal, and I wouldn't have had to face trying to resolve a problem I had generated.*

Initially, you can work on thinking up alternative and healthier behaviours after the event. This will allow you to learn how to make better choices by considering the different outcomes of various behaviours. It will then become easier to apply this strategy when you feel the emotional reaction so that you can choose the better behaviour at the time and avoid doing things that might feel all right at the time but do not help you in the longer term. Below is a worksheet you can use.

The emotion-behaviour link worksheet	
I feel/felt…	
I did/I felt the urge to do…	
What happened/ what would have happened?	
A better choice…	
Likely outcome…	

Worksheet available at elemen.com.au

It might be worthwhile next to give some additional assistance with the particularly difficult emotional response of anger. As this is the emotion that drives many of our poor behaviour choices, it is sensible to learn some additional skills.

Managing your anger

It should be noted that there are times when your increased nervous system arousal will manifest as an angry response rather than an anxious one. You might find yourself raising your voice or becoming overwhelmed by frustration and annoyance. You might act out in ways that you would not do if you were in a calmer state of mind. Certainly, at these times, you can act in a way that does not make you feel good about yourself when you reflect on what you have done.

For someone who feels a strong need to be in control, anger can be a frequently experienced emotional response. Anger flares when your need to be in control is frustrated.

If you have a more significant anger control problem, then we recommend that you seek a workbook that focuses on more extensive ways in which you can learn to control your anger or seek out professional help. However, here we would like to focus on some simple ideas that may help you control your angry feelings. Firstly, we will teach you a simple strategy to manage an angry response.

To understand why this strategy is effective, you need to consider that anger tends to be experienced in an escalating manner. That is, an angry response is triggered and then gets worse when one or both of two things happen. The first is that you can think anger-provoking thoughts that will build your anger. These thoughts tend to relate to things not being the way you want them to be and your feeling that what you are experiencing is not justified and should not be happening.

The second refers to a process of reaction to how the other person responds to your anger that escalates the angry interaction. That is, an initial angry comment can be made, and the other person then becomes angry, so you become more angry, and then the other person's anger increases further. This escalating pattern leads to uncontrolled anger.

So, what should you do if you find your anger being triggered or your anger escalating?

Exit and wait strategy

The most straightforward strategy you can use to stop the escalation of your anger and allow it to abate is an exit and wait strategy. When you are feeling angry, leave the situation and wait until you are calm before you return. It is an easy and effective strategy. Walk out of the room and allow yourself to calm down.

This exit and wait strategy is not about you backing down or giving in. Indeed, it is a strategy that allows you to take control of an escalating situation and manage it in a way to ensure that ensures a better outcome than would have been experienced had you let the angry situation develop.

When away from the anger-provoking situation, there are a couple of tips you can use to help you calm down more quickly. Firstly, avoid going over the angry situation in your mind. This only aggravates your anger and makes it harder for you to settle down. So, when you leave the room, try to think about something else. Distract yourself by focusing on something that will hold your attention. Secondly, you can physically control your angry reaction by slowing your breathing and relaxing your tense muscles. This allows you to bring your nervous system over-arousal under control.

When you are calm and better able to handle the situation, return to what you were doing when the angry response was triggered. Go back with the right frame of mind. Decide that you are going to disengage from the interaction that caused the problem. You can adopt a spectator role by simply observing what you are doing without interpreting and judging. This will help you to continue while reducing the risk of further escalations of anger. Adopting a spectator role in an interaction is a useful way of disengaging from the emotional response that is not proving useful for you.

Controlling thoughts that trigger anger

While the exit and wait technique is an emergency control strategy, you may need something more complex to effectively deal with your angry feelings. We can start by examining the types of thoughts that trigger angry feelings.

In a general sense, angry thoughts are triggered by a particular point of view that serves to justify our right to be angry. This point of view is made up of the following thought combination:

> I have been harmed or victimised by the other person.
>
> This person harmed me or victimised me deliberately.
>
> This person should not have done this; they were wrong; they should have chosen to act differently and in a way that would not harm or victimise me.

These thoughts tend to underlie most angry interactions. If you broke your angry thoughts into their particular elements, you would be able to discern the following:

> The harm done.
>
> The way it was done deliberately.
>
> Why this was wrong.

However, it should be remembered that this is your *perception* of the situation rather than the *facts* of the situation. How right or wrong you are in your perception is not determined by what you see as your justifiable anger. That is, your anger does not make these things true. Rightness or wrongness will be determined by the facts of the matter.

Unfortunately, it is hard to consider the facts when you are in an angry state. In effect, you are blinded by your emotional state and not in a position to think things through clearly. Your anger makes you want to push your point of view, even when, on calm reflection, you may see that your point is not a good one.

Also, even if it is the case that someone has done the wrong thing, it does not mean that you cannot choose what way you will respond to this. It does not follow that you have to feel anger in response to someone else's actions. For example, you may choose to just shrug your shoulders about their behaviour and ignore their attempts to rile you.

Instead of just focusing on the situation that triggered your anger, you may be better served to think of ways that would allow you to manage how you respond. This allows you to take responsibility for the outcome rather than being a helpless victim of someone else's poor behaviour. Consider the following example.

Changing my reaction – Example 1
What happened to provoke my anger? *I was in a meeting at work, and we were discussing changes that needed to be made to our procedures. The others ignored my ideas and went with someone else's suggestions.*
How did I interpret this event? *I interpreted this as them deliberately disregarding my point of view, even though they should have been able to see that my ideas were better than the ones they chose.*
What did I think should happen? *I think they should have done things my way and gone along with my ideas.*
How could I think differently about this situation? *I could see that sometimes they agreed with my ideas, and sometimes they agreed with someone else's ideas. I could see that the preferred option is the one that the majority of people agree with and, in this case, that was someone else's ideas. I could see that if these new procedures didn't work out, we could always make further adjustments.*
How is this likely to make me feel? *I would feel disappointed they didn't choose my ideas but I wouldn't be angry. I would feel accepting of the fact that it was not my turn for my ideas to be taken on board. I could feel confident that nothing terrible will happen just because they accepted someone else's ideas.*

Let's consider another example.

Changing my reaction – Example 2
What happened to provoke my anger? *I had given my partner a list of jobs to do while I was at work, but they had not completed all of the tasks by the time I returned home.*
How did I interpret this event? *I believed my partner had chosen to be lazy and had deliberately disregarded my wishes.*
What did I think should happen? *I think my partner should have worked harder and completed all the tasks I set.*
How could I think differently about this situation? *I could see that my list of tasks was a list of requests and not demands that I should expect someone else to comply with. I could see that although it would have been good to get the jobs done, most were not so urgent that they had to be done that day. I could acknowledge that my partner had done some of the things on the list and been grateful for their effort.*
How is this likely to make me feel? *I might have been disappointed that all the tasks had not been completed, but I would not have felt angry. I can handle being disappointed.*

It is a good idea for you to work through your reactions to anger-provoking situations to see if you can re-interpret them in a way that helps you manage your angry feelings. It is worth keeping in mind that angry feelings can be unpleasant and can drive you to do things that you might not choose to do if you were calmer. You can use the worksheet below to go through this process of reframing your response to anger-provoking situations.

Changing my reaction worksheet
What happened to provoke my anger?
How did I interpret this event?
What did I think should happen?
How could I think differently about this situation?
How is this likely to make me feel?

Worksheet available at elemen.com.au

If your angry reactions are just a reflection of the situation you are in, then these steps should help you manage those reactions and help you choose to react differently and in a way that is advantageous to you. This can help you settle your nervous system and feel calmer. Certainly, without reactive anger, you can begin to think differently and more clearly about your situation.

Learning acceptance

To cope with overwhelming emotional states, such as those that can develop when you are driven by a strong need to be in control, it is necessary to learn ways to manage the distress you feel when things do not work out the way you want.

A change of attitude

Typically, when stressful events occur, we react to them in the context of something being done to us or happening to us. If we hold someone else responsible, then we tend to react with anger and resentment, holding the view that the person involved should have done something other than what they did. If we hold ourselves responsible, then we tend to focus on self-criticism and regret. The result is that we start a battle within ourselves in relation to the event. The more we focus on our anger and resentment, or our self-criticism and regret, the more distressed we tend to feel in relation to our experiences that triggered these feelings.

The trouble with this approach is that it does not really let us accept and deal with the fact that the event has actually happened and that we must cope with it… because we have little choice. We focus more on the past, which we cannot change, and give less attention to the present and the future, over which we can exert some influence.

When you are dealing with situations where you try to exert control, you are faced with challenges. Most of these challenges are not things you would choose to have happen. This can cause you to experience distress when the challenges occur and even after they occur in situations when things do not work out the way you wish.

To cope with this, you need to consider a change in attitude to one of acceptance rather than being tormented by events that you cannot change. There are lots of things that can happen that cause you pain and emotional upset. The more you focus on these situations, the more distress you tend to feel. The goal here is to learn to accept the things you cannot change.

Often, when we have to deal with a change we did not want or things happening differently from what we would expect, we tend to get upset, thinking that this is something that should not have happened or should not have happened to us in particular. Rather than battle events that have already occurred in this way, the goal is to accept that they *did* happen and that it is now appropriate for you to deal with these changed situations.

Being distressed about a situation does not help you cope with that situation. It is a fact that you cannot change the past. Nevertheless, we tend to emotionally react to these situations as if there is something we can do to change them. In doing this, you become stuck and do not look for other, more effective ways of coping with your new circumstance.

In learning acceptance, you need to acknowledge your changed situation without trying to control it or change things that have already happened. Try to understand that your current situation has occurred because there was a long chain of events that occurred in the past that brought you to this point. Your job now is to use your coping skills to move forward with life, as it is a waste of your energy and effort to torment yourself thinking "if only…" or "what if…".

This type of acceptance does not mean that you cannot wish that things had turned out differently. It also does not stop you from looking for ways to manage or improve your current situation or avoid things that might happen in the future. This type of acceptance is asking you to look at your situation and accept it for what it is. It is from here that you can then choose what you want to do about it.

Whenever you feel overwhelmed by your situation, you can use simple coping statements that will remind you that a position of acceptance is preferable. Consider the following coping statements. Add anything that you can think of that would help you accept what has happened so that you can move forward and deal with things as they arise.

Acceptance coping statements	
Below are some examples of coping statements that would help you achieve acceptance. These coping statements remind you to accept your situation and the events that contributed to your current situation. Tick the coping statements that you would find useful, and then add any others you believe will help. Then, when you feel overwhelmed, use these coping statements to help you manage your reaction to the events that are stressing you.	
	Things are the way they are.
	There is a chain of things that contributed to what is happening now.
	I cannot change things that have already happened.
	There is no point battling past events.
	Battling the past upsets my present.
	I can only deal with the present.
	It is a waste of my energy to try to change the past.
	The present is as it should be, even if it is not what I would choose.
	This moment in time has occurred because of all the things that came before.

Add your own coping statements

Worksheet available at elemen.com.au

These coping statements can remind you to stop fighting a past you cannot change. This will free you up to accept what has happened and then focus your energy on moving forward and doing what is best for you. Acceptance of what has happened invites you to cope with what you are experiencing.

Of course, when someone is trying to exert control over all events, it is not only the past when things did not work out as anticipated that will be the focus of your attention. You will also try to control the future by anticipating what might happen and having control strategies that will convince you that the future is manageable. In effect, this will mean that you may worry about things in the future over which you do not have control because you cannot know what will happen.

Worry control strategies

To understand how worry works, let's consider the simplified version of a worry model in the diagram below. You experience intrusive worry thoughts that come into your mind even when you do not want to think about these things. These relate to possible future threats to yourself or others you care about. Then, a cycle of worry develops where you keep re-evaluating the threat, reaching the same conclusion that the threat is real or possibly real. No matter how many times you go over it, the threat continues to play on your mind. Of course, this causes you to feel anxious.

Here, we are going to focus on a simple worry control strategy that will help you deal with your worrying by attempting to interrupt that cycle of worry. In effect, the cycle of worry causes you to feel anxious, which causes you to worry more, which causes you to feel more anxious. You need to step away from this cycle.

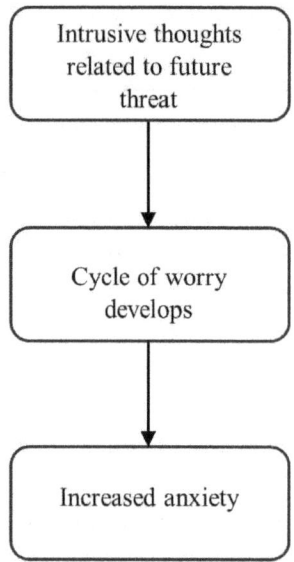

Figure 7: A diagram of the cycle of worry.

Looking more closely at this cycle of worry, what you do when you are worrying is outlined in the diagram below. When you have intrusive thoughts about a potential problem situation, you make some attempts to control that worry. Of course, if you could control your worry, you would simply do that. As a result of the worry being unpleasant, you search for some relief. But, all your control efforts to stop this process fail, and your worry remains. You then start to worry that you are worrying. You then go back to trying to control your worry... and so on.

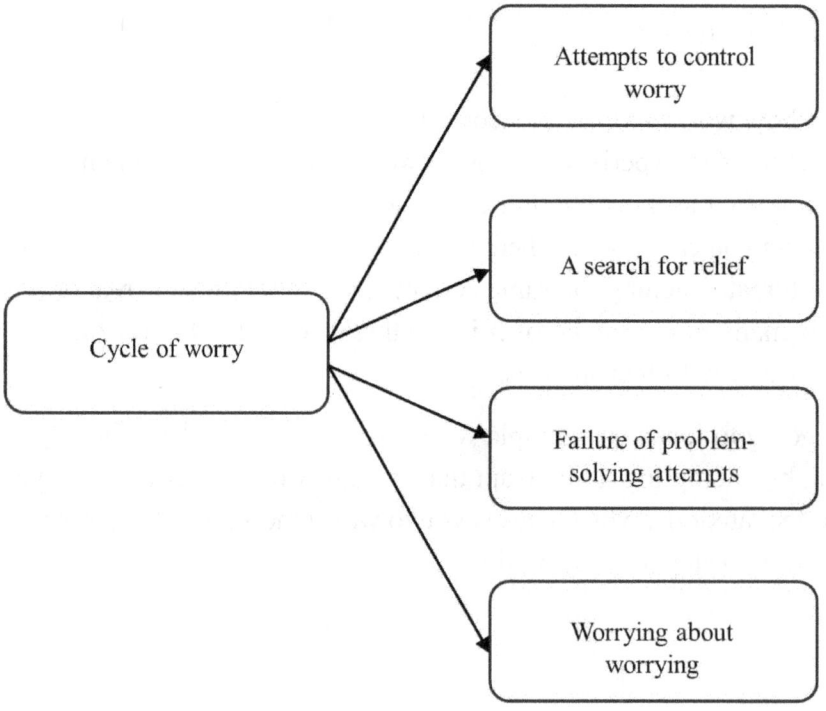

Figure 8: The components of the cycle of worry.

A simple strategy to manage worry

To help manage worry, you need to break the cycle of worry that leads to feelings of anxiety. Below is a simple strategy to manage your worrying. It seems too simple to be effective, but it has proved successful for many people.

	Allocating worry time
1.	Allocate a 15-minute period of your day for worrying. You choose the time that is more effective for you. For the purposes of this exercise, let's say you allocate 5.00-5.15 pm as your worry time.
2.	During the day, catch yourself having worry thoughts. As soon as you notice you are worrying, acknowledge that you are worrying and tell yourself the following, "I will worry about that during my worry time, at 5.00pm". Then deliberately move your thoughts to something else.
3.	Do this as often as you catch yourself worrying. Do not be concerned that when you start doing this, you will probably catch yourself worrying many times. Just remember that each time you notice you are worrying, remind yourself that you will worry about it at your allocated time and then move on to thinking about something else.
4.	When your allocated time arrives, you have permission to worry as much as you like for 15 minutes. However, you do not have to do this. Most often, people will not be bothered. You may also find that it is actually quite difficult to deliberately worry for 15 minutes. That is ok. You do not have to worry if you do not want to.

Exercise available at elemen.com.au

This will help stop the escalation of your worrying that leads to anxious feelings.

There is one more important issue we need to address. We need to consider the way we think and how this affects how we feel and what we do.

Changing your thinking

To feel better, we might have to change the way we view something so that we are not vulnerable to distressed reactions to events that have already happened and/or potential situations in the future that we cannot control. Let's think of ways we can challenge unhelpful thinking and replace it with the types of thoughts that allow us to see things more clearly and choose behaviours that will help us.

How are our thoughts affected?

As we go through life, we can develop unhelpful thinking styles or errors in our thinking. These errors influence how we interpret the world around us and how we fit into that world. In an attempt to make sense of the world, we develop 'templates' or models of how we think things should work.

For example, you might develop a template that tells you that you have to be the best at everything you do. On the surface, this seems workable. You just have to work hard and keep things in your control. However, if you have a template that you have to be the best, what happens when someone does better than you? You then become upset about something that really is an ordinary enough experience. You then feel like you are not worthwhile, even in situations where you tried your hardest to succeed. We have met lots of people who want to succeed. Unfortunately, your template might tell you that to be a worthwhile person, you *must* be the best in all areas of your life. You can see the problem.

Our individual templates are put together based on information from a variety of sources, including, for example, our personality and our experiences throughout life. If the messages we receive from our experiences in life are good and healthy ones, we tend to have good and healthy templates of how the world works and how we fit into that world. However, if the messages are distorted in some way (e.g., being told you have to be the best at everything you do, that no one will like you if you disagree with them, your needs are not as important as other people's needs), then the template we develop will reflect these messages and will be unhelpful.

Core beliefs

So, how does this template affect us? It tells us how we should respond when dealing with our world and the people in it. The information we gather throughout our life determines our 'core beliefs' about three things:

> How safe or dangerous we perceived the world to be.
>
> Our place in that world and our value as a person.
>
> How certain the future feels.

These core beliefs are not the 'truth' of things. They develop as a result of the information we gather along the way in life, whether or not that information is helpful or unhelpful, clear or confusing, or accurate or distorted.

If we have helpful, clear and accurate templates, then our core beliefs are healthy, and our thinking does not contain errors about how the world works and how we fit into that world. However, if we have unhelpful, confusing and distorted templates, our thinking contains errors that affect how we react to the world and how we view ourselves in that world.

Cognitive errors

Cognitive errors are the errors in thinking that occur when our templates of how the world works and how we fit into that world send us the wrong message. Our thinking about our experiences is then altered by the wrong message. Problems arise when we engage in certain types of cognitive errors.

Below are some of the most common cognitive errors. As you read through them, think about whether these types of errors occur in your thinking.

Table 2: Descriptions of the common errors in thinking.

Types of errors of thinking	
Error type	*Error in thinking*
Filtering	A person whose thinking is affected by filtering takes the negative details of an event and exaggerates them while filtering out any positive aspects of the situation. For example, the person who would not eat the meal her partner prepared focused on the fact that he did not prepare it as she instructed. She ignored the fact that her husband often cooked tasty meals that she enjoyed, that it was nice that she had a meal prepared for her, and that she had extra time to herself because her partner was cooking.
Polarised thinking	With polarised thinking, things are either 'black or white' or 'all or nothing'. People who think this way place situations in 'either/or' categories, with no middle ground to account for the complexity of most situations. For example, a person with a strong need to be in control might believe that people at work have to do things their way or else things are being done the wrong way. There is no opportunity for collaborative problem-solving and no occasion when consideration is given to other people's ideas.

Overgeneralisation	A person makes a conclusion based on one event or a single piece of information. In this way, if something bad happens to them on one occasion, they expect it to happen over and over again. For example, on one occasion, when people rejected her plans and things did not go well, this person came to expect things always to go poorly if people did not do as she demanded.
Jumping to conclusions	If a person jumps to conclusions, they 'know' what the other person is thinking about without that person saying so. For example, a person may become annoyed because they 'know' that the person they are trying to control understands that they are right but is just refusing to acknowledge it.
Catastrophising	A person who catastrophises expects disaster to strike, no matter what. A person hears about a problem and uses *what-if* questions to imagine the worst outcome. For example, a person who likes to control everything believes that terrible things will happen if others do not do what they demand.
Personalisation	A person believes that everything others do or say is some kind of direct, personal reaction to them. They take everything personally. For example, a refusal by others to adopt their plans may lead a controlling person to believe that others are doing that deliberately as an act of revenge.
Control fallacies	This occurs when a person strongly endorses the view that they must be in control of all situations. This can occur in two ways. Firstly, there is external control, where the person feels they are a helpless victim of fate, and secondly, internal control, where a person assumes responsibility for the pain and unhappiness of others. For example, a person who likes to be in control might believe they are responsible for other people's unhappiness if they are unsuccessful in taking charge of everything and 'ensuring' a good outcome.

Fallacy of fairness	A person who believes they know what is fair will feel resentful and unhappy if others disagree with them. People who judge every event in their lives in terms of whether or not it is fair will often feel resentful, angry and hopeless. For example, a person who likes to be in control may view it as unfair that others refuse to accept their good intentions and well-meaning plans and, instead, reject their controlling ways.
Blaming	This person holds other people responsible for their own emotional pain. Alternatively, they may blame themselves for every problem – even those clearly outside their control. For example, a person who likes to be in control may attribute their own unhappiness to other people's rejection of their best efforts to effect good outcomes by being in charge of every course of action.
Shoulds	Should statements (e.g., I should visit my parents more) are made by people who hold rigid rules about how the world should work and how everyone should behave. Breaking these rules makes a person angry. They also feel guilty when they violate their own rules. For example, a person who likes to be in control might believe that everyone should do what they say and do it their way, with no exceptions.
Emotional reasoning	People with this distortion in thinking are guided by what they 'feel' is the truth. They will rely on their feelings to establish whether or not something is 'fact'. If a person feels unworthy, then they must be unworthy. Emotional reasoning blocks rationality and logic. For example, a person who needs to be in control may believe they are the best person to be in charge because it makes them feel anxious when they are not in charge. Because they feel calmer when they are in charge, they believe that being in charge is absolutely the right thing to do.
Fallacy of change	A person with this type of thinking will believe that if they apply enough pressure, others will change to meet their needs. This person needs others to change because they cannot cope if others disagree with them or behave in ways that are contrary to how this person feels they should behave. For example, a person who likes to feel in control may pressure others to do what they demand because they believe they cannot be happy and anxiety-free unless people do what they want.

Global labelling	A person generalises a small number of features or characteristics of themselves or others and inflates them into a global statement or judgment. This goes beyond overgeneralising. Rather than take into account the context of a situation, the person will apply this judgment to all aspects of a person or situation. For example, because others often refuse to do what this person says they must, they label them as insightless, recalcitrant, and foolish despite these people otherwise being viewed as reasonable.
Always being right	When a person engages in this error of thinking, they insist that all views held by them or actions done by them are correct. In their view, they cannot make a mistake or be misinformed. For someone with a strong need to be in control, this person may push and demand others to agree with them and do as they insist and reject any indication that they are not absolutely right.
Heaven's reward fallacy	A person who engages in this type of thinking believes that a person's hard work and sacrifice will pay off in the end as if someone is keeping track of what everyone does in life. Sharing some similarities with the fallacy of fairness thinking, this person believes that the one who does the most, works the hardest or sacrifices the most will be the person who is rewarded at some point in the future. For example, a person who likes to be in control will be confused and unhappy when others reject them because this person believes that what they are doing is for the best of everyone.

Let's consider how these errors in thinking affect a person's point of view. Below are examples of these types of logical errors in thinking, along with a more rational point of view.

Table 3: Examples of rational and irrational perspectives for each error in thinking.

Correcting your thinking	
Error in thinking	*A rational view*
Filtering	
Joel had been working on a project at work. He had full control of the project and this suited him well. Joel's boss was pleased with his progress but thought Joel had too much to do. His boss decided to take one part of the project and give it to another employee to complete. Joel was very upset. He focused only on his boss, telling him he could not be expected to do everything. Joe concluded that his boss was not happy with his performance, and he concluded that the control of the project had been taken away from him.	Instead of being pleased with the praise that was offered by his boss and the decision to lighten his load, Joel could only focus on what he saw as losing control of his project. He saw this as a poor reflection of his abilities. He would have been better off seeing that the provision of assistance on the project was a reflection of his boss' understanding of how much work he had been doing.
Polarised thinking	
Stuart was a member of an engineering team at his place of work. Stuart had very definite views about how things should be done. If things were not done his way, Stuart would become angry and disrupt the smooth running of the team's projects. The team leader decided a more collaborative approach was needed and informed Stuart that, although he appreciated his input, other people's ideas would be taken into account. Stuart asked to be moved to a different team. He believed that the functioning of the team had irretrievably broken down. In his view, either his ideas were always taken into account, or the team simply was not working.	Stuart should have realised that a collaborative approach to teamwork is not the same thing as a breakdown of team functioning. Indeed, it is the opposite. In understanding that this is how teams should work, Stuart would have been able to see that he could have had more influence on the team by advocating for his own proposals and ideas without demanding that others oblige him. A more moderate view would have allowed the team to work and Stuart to see himself as a valuable member of that team.

Overgeneralisation	
Sophie's daughter accused her of interfering in her life. It certainly was the case that Sophie tried to control her daughter's life even though her daughter was a young adult. Early on in her daughter's adolescence, Sophie's daughter made poor choices and got into trouble. Sophie intervened, and the situation was managed. Sophie then concluded that without her influence in her life, her daughter would continue to make mistakes. So, Sophie went to excessive lengths to control her daughter, going outside of the family to both gain information about her daughter and take control by making decisions for her. Sophie's daughter was understandably angry.	Sophie has made the mistake of believing that because her daughter made one mistake and she had to intervene, her daughter will continue to make mistakes, justifying Sophie's control of her daughter's life. Sophie should realise that most teenagers learn from their earlier mistakes and give her daughter the opportunity to demonstrate this learning rather than just assuming that her daughter will always make mistakes.
Jumping to conclusions	
Rebecca's colleague at work made a minor and inconsequential mistake. The boss brushed off the importance of this error. However, Rebecca made an issue of the matter, blaming her colleague for failing to do as she directed just because her colleague refused to accept Rebecca's superior knowledge. Rebecca concluded that she 'knew' that her colleague was refusing to accept that Rebecca knew best just because she did not want to admit that Rebecca was right.	Rather than jumping to the conclusion that she knew best, that her colleague knew this to be the case, and that her colleague was deliberately refusing to accept these facts, Rebecca would have been better off accepting some simple truths. Firstly, everyone makes mistakes from time to time, including Rebecca, and secondly, that the mistake was inconsequential and deemed unimportant by the boss. The result would have been that Rebecca was considered to be a supportive colleague rather than a demanding one. The likelihood of interpersonal difficulties between Rebecca and others would have been reduced.

Catastrophising	
Patricia would lay awake at night worrying about what was going to happen in the future. Her husband simply refused to accept that she knew what was best for them. As a consequence, Patricia believed they were facing financial struggles because her husband would not see sense. Patricia's friends pointed out to her that she and her husband seemed to be in a good financial state and that the things she was concerned about were unlikely to happen. Nevertheless, Patricia thought that because things were not being done her way, only bad things would eventuate.	Patricia could not see any future other than the one she had predicted, believing that the failure of her husband to hand over management of their financial situation would result in disaster. Patricia would have been better off sitting down with an advisor who could look at the facts and reach an objective conclusion about their financial future. Certainly, the advice she had received so far and rejected indicated that her future was sound. With a proper examination of the objective facts, Patricia may have been able to feel less stressed about the future she assumed would be terrible.

Personalisation	
John's friends decided to go to a concert at the weekend. John wanted to go camping with his friends. An argument of sorts developed. His friends tried to explain that the concert was a one-off opportunity and they could go camping any other weekend. But John wanted to go camping this weekend. He was not interested in the concert. John thought that his friends were doing this deliberately to upset him. He could not believe that his friends would reject his idea to go camping for any reason other than to make him unhappy. John was angry about them treating him so poorly.	John's friends had a legitimate reason for rejecting his plans in favour of their own. A one-off opportunity had arisen for them to attend a concert. However, John had taken their rejection personally. Rather than it being a matter of timing and opportunity, John believed their actions were deliberately hurtful to him. John would have benefitted by seeing that sometimes our plans are thwarted for reasons other than personal attacks. This may have caused him to feel less aggrieved about his friends' decision to do other than what he wanted.

Control fallacies	
Andrea always took it upon herself to organise Christmas celebrations for her family. Every year she was the one who made all the plans, cooked, decorated her home, purchased presents for everyone and arranged all the activities. This undertaking was always anxiety-provoking for her, exhausting and expensive. Andrea could not trust anyone else to do this for her. She thought that if she took control of everything, she could ensure her family members' happiness and enjoyment of the celebration. For Andrea, it was a huge burden of responsibility, but she felt that she had no choice because she wanted her family to be happy.	Andrea is making a mistake in assuming that she can control the happiness of her individual family members. She would have been better off realising that each individual is in charge of their own feelings, including their own happiness. Whether they are happy would not be solely determined by the effort she spends in controlling the celebrations. She could have done less and allowed others to participate in the process and still have a good outcome.
Fallacy of fairness	
Jacqueline volunteered at a local charitable organisation. She worked hard and was dedicated to what she was doing to help others. However, she liked things being done her way. The other volunteers did not like being told what to do. They asked not to be rostered on with Jacqueline. Jacqueline thought it was very unfair that the other volunteers treated her this way and rejected her good ideas about more effective performance in their tasks. She thought that if she worked hard, other people would appreciate her efforts.	Jacqueline has made a mistake in thinking that her hard work will cause people to treat her in a way she considers fair. She failed to understand that there were aspects of her behaviour that people resented that were not related to how hard she worked as a volunteer. In any case, believing that certain things should happen because they are fair disregards the fact that the world is neither fair nor unfair. It would have helped Jacqueline to disregard this belief of fairness. This might have allowed her to consider what she was doing that was making people so resentful and then correct that behaviour.

Blaming	
Jack blamed his wife for his unhappiness. He knew he would be happy in life if his wife would just recognise that he knew what was best for them. He resented the fact that she would disagree with him and do things in ways other than he directed. Jack often complained to his wife that she was making him unhappy. He said it was all her fault and that she could easily rectify the situation if she just accepted that he knew best.	Jack's wife was not responsible for his unhappiness. In fact, Jack's expectation that things in life should go his way is the thing that is causing his unhappiness. By blaming his wife, Jack does not have to do anything to change his own expectations and behaviour. Jack could take control of his own emotional state by adjusting his expectations of others.
Shoulds	
Craig was a member of the board of directors of a not-for-profit organisation. The organisation was going through a period of restructuring that was being overseen by the board. A full-on argument between board members had developed. Craig kept telling other board members that they must do things the way he saw them working. Some board members were willing to give Craig what he wanted to avoid conflict. However, others were resistant to Craig's ideas, seeing problems that Craig was unwilling to acknowledge. Craig believed all board members should do as he said. He saw it as their obligation if they had a goal of a smooth-running organisation. Craig could not see that there might be other ways of doing things.	Craig was failing to see that other people could have opinions other than his own. He believed that, for things to work, they had to be done his way. He did not even stop to consider other options. Craig could avoid conflict if he could moderate his thinking from believing that others should do as he says to accept that collaborative decision-making can work.

Emotional reasoning

Suzanne had organised a weekend away with some old friends. She had made extensive plans for the trip. However, some of her plans went wrong. She had rented a property for the weekend, and the person who was to meet them to hand over the keys arrived late. A nearby restaurant where Suzanne had planned to take her friends to dinner was closed unexpectedly. Suzanne had wanted a sun-filled weekend, but the weather was not very good.

Despite her friends being happy and enjoying the weekend, the problems Suzanne did not anticipate made her anxious. She reached the conclusion that it had been a disaster of a weekend.

When things do not go as Suzanne expects and demands, she feels anxious. That anxious feeling on the weekend away caused Suzanne to form the view that the weekend was terrible and unenjoyable. Her feelings resulted in her believing there was a problem. However, if she had been able to look at the objective indicators that a problem was or was not present, she would have been able to see that her friends had enjoyed themselves and the minor problems she could not control were insignificant. If her friends were happy and there really were no significant problems, then there was no reason to be anxious.

Fallacy of change

Andre was never very comfortable talking about his feelings. In contrast, his girlfriend, Lisa, loved to talk about how she was feeling and to dissect every interaction she had with Andre to understand its meaning. Lisa constantly pressured Andre to engage in intense and exhausting discussions about how Andre felt about even the tiniest thing. Lisa thought this was the right thing to do and insisted that Andre get on board with her decision.

Lisa thought all their relationship problems would be resolved if Andre would just do as she asked and talked about how he was feeling.

Lisa has made the mistake of assuming that because she values something, everyone else should value it, too. Andre is expected to change to meet her needs. Lisa is upset because she believes Andre is deliberately withholding something from her. She fails to see that she is upsetting herself by expecting something of Andre that he is not able to provide.

Global labelling	
Ian would come home at night and complain about his colleagues at work. He would go over with his wife all the occasions that day that his colleagues had failed to agree with him, not done as he wanted or made agreements with others than disregarded his ideas. In Ian's telling of his problems, his colleagues were insightless and 'stupid'. He believed he was the only reasonable person in his workplace and the only one with good ideas. Ian's wife disagreed with his view of his colleagues, but she dared not say so. Ian was already stressed enough, and she knew that challenging him would only aggravate his emotional state.	With being unable to cope with things not working out the way he wants, Ian is making himself miserable. By focusing on his colleagues' refusal to do what he says, he is failing to consider the value of their suggestions and the way they do things. As a result, he makes global statements about their lack of worth. This is a problem. If he labels his colleagues as stupid, then he will treat them as such and fail to view them in a more flexible way. If he avoided this global labelling, he may be able to work more collaboratively with his colleagues.
Always being right	
Brad was struggling with his wife Olivia's tendency to refuse to let go of any argument. Silly disagreements with Olivia would escalate into full-blown arguments because she had to be right. If he tried to walk away from the argument, she would follow him and demand that he acknowledge she was right. Weeks down the track, Olivia would bring up issues Brad had thought had been resolved and would insist that he admit she had been right all along. Brad has been exhausted by this whole process and was questioning the workability of their relationship. Olivia could not understand why Brad just did not accept what was obvious, that is, that she was right.	Olivia is causing a problem by believing the only way to feel emotionally comfortable is to be proven to be right. She has failed to understand that other people may not share her opinions. She also has failed to understand that it is possible to feel ok even if people do not agree with her. Olivia would be better off emotionally if she could accept that differences of opinion need not result in ongoing conflict. She cannot change other people's opinions to align them with her own by force of will.

Heaven's reward fallacy	
Chloe's sisters have distanced themselves from Chloe and she is confused about their reasons for doing so. Chloe has done lots of things for her sisters. She has looked after their children, helped in their garden, loaned them money in the past, cooked for them and helped them with their housework when they are unwell. The problem for the sisters is not what Chloe has done for them. Their problem is how controlling and bossy Chloe is when she involves herself in their lives. Yes, she has helped them, but only if they do things the way Chloe wants. She continually tells them where they are going wrong and disregards their wishes when she comes into their homes. They say Chloe is like a bulldozer in her determination to have things done the way she wants.	Chloe has made the mistake of believing that because she has done good things for others, then everyone will treat her nicely. She thinks their withdrawal from her is unwarranted given how helpful she has been. Chloe needs to realise that doing good things for others does not offer a guarantee that others will reward you. She would do better to consider why she is being rejected rather than feelings resentful that her efforts are unappreciated.

It is apparent that these types of logical errors do not make things easy for us. Quite the opposite. They lead us to misinterpret events so that we adopt a limited or negative perspective that colours how we view things, our emotional responses, and the choices of how we behave as a consequence.

Why do we think in unhelpful ways?

Why do we think in ways that are distorted and not particularly helpful? To understand why errors in thinking happen, we have to consider the theory behind cognitive behaviour therapy (CBT). According to this theory, our thinking has more than one level. This is displayed in the diagram below.

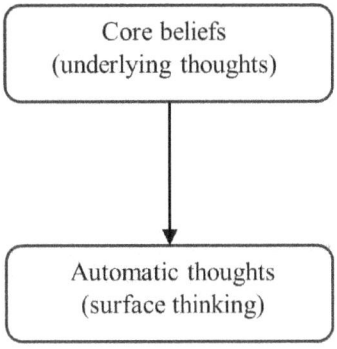

Figure 9: A diagram of the two levels of thought.

Automatic thoughts refer to the running commentary that goes through our heads as we go about our daily lives. If you pay attention, you will notice the constant chatter that goes on in your head about the things you are doing and how you are reacting to the people and events around you.

There is an easy exercise that will show you how this running commentary works. For the next minute, think about a bowl of fruit. Over the course of the minute, just let your thoughts do what they want as you think about a bowl of fruit. At the end of the minute, notice where your thoughts have taken you. Now consider the links between your starting point (thinking about a bowl of fruit) and where you ended up (thinking whatever it was you were thinking). Consider below how this might have played out for one individual. This person started thinking about a bowl of fruit and ended up thinking about cleaning out their pantry. Follow their automatic thoughts.

> *Ok. I'm thinking about a bowl of fruit. I can picture a bowl of fruit. It's got bananas in it. I like bananas. I should buy some next time I go to the supermarket. I also need to get a loaf of bread. I must start a shopping list. Pay attention and think about a bowl of fruit. Oh, and milk, I mustn't forget milk. I hate running out of milk. Someone said once that they have orange juice on their cereal instead of milk. Yuck. I couldn't imagine anything worse. Not that I eat much cereal. I should eat more cereal... it's probably good for you. I will put cereal on my shopping list. But that might be a waste because I probably won't eat it. I have bought lots of things I thought would be good for me, but I never ate them. That reminds me that I should clean out the pantry.*

Core beliefs refer to the underlying beliefs we have about how the world works and how we fit into that world. Core beliefs have influence on our automatic thoughts. That is, we think the things we do on the surface because of our underlying beliefs about how things work. Unlike automatic thoughts, the content of our core beliefs is not readily available to us but can be examined by considering the content of our automatic thoughts.

So, where do the logical errors in thinking we have been talking about fit into this conceptualisation? Let's consider that in the diagram below.

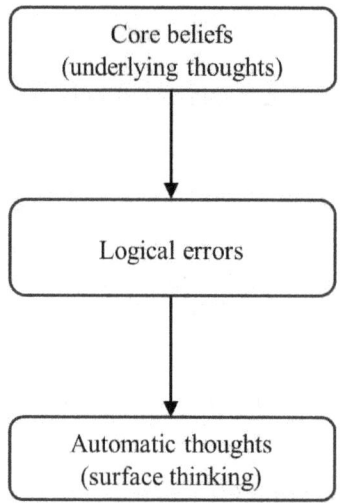

Figure 10: Where errors in thinking occur in our levels of thought.

The errors in thinking we make are a result of the core beliefs we hold. For example, if our core beliefs about the world and the future are that the world is threatening and the outlook is grim and pessimistic, then we are likely to inflate the degree of dangerousness we perceive and we are likely to catastrophise.

These logical errors then affect our surface thinking. We are more likely to be self-critical or tell ourselves everything is hopeless or tell ourselves that nothing is fair because of the logical errors we make based on our particular core beliefs.

Our core beliefs are built on the basis of a variety of influences. These include our genetic makeup (e.g., an inherited overly reactive nervous system), our experiences (the things that happen to us), the messages we receive (the things people have said to us or the way they have treated us), and the ways we have interpreted these events. If the influences are positive and healthy, our core beliefs tend to be clear, and there are few logical errors. If the influences on us are negative, unhealthy or confusing, our core beliefs tend to be inaccurate, and the logical errors we make are many and strongly influence our automatic thoughts.

Underlying assumptions of logical errors

It has been suggested that each logical error is driven by specific assumptions. If our automatic thoughts are biased, then the biases are driven by our core beliefs and assumptions. Below are some examples of cognitive errors and examples of associated assumptions. Here we are referring to the assumptions that are inevitably made if the errors in our thinking are present.

Table 4: The assumptions underlying each logical error.

Cognitive error	Assumption
Filtering	The only events that matter are failures. I should measure myself by my errors.
Polarised thinking	Everything is always one extreme or the other.
Overgeneralisation	If it's true in one case, it must be true in every case that is even slightly similar.
Jumping to conclusions	If it has always been true in the past, it is going to be true in the future.
Catastrophising	Always think the worst because it is most likely to happen to you.
Personalisation	I am responsible for all bad things, failures, etc.
Control fallacies	You should be able to know in advance what is going to happen. When, after the event, you understand the chain of events that resulted in a bad thing happening, this means that you should have seen the bad thing coming before it happened.
Fallacy of fairness	The world is a fair place and fairness will influence how things turn out.
Blaming	Whether it is me or someone else, someone is always responsible when things are not the way I want them to be.
Shoulds	People have an obligation to do specific things that cannot be avoided.
Emotional reasoning	If a person feels bad, something must be wrong.
Fallacy of change	People must change to meet other people's needs.
Global labelling	A whole person and their entire life can be summed up by a single word (e.g., stupid).

Always being right	People have to choose a side, and there is a right side and a wrong side.
Heaven's reward fallacy	Choosing to do good things for others will oblige others to do good things in return.

Let's consider how these logical errors and the assumptions that are made affect automatic thoughts. Consider in this example what this person is saying to themselves about a situation they were trying to control but could not control.

> *I can't believe it. My daughter just told me she and her husband are putting their house on the market with the intention of moving to the country. I told her not to do this. I told her what happened to her aunt all those years ago when she moved away from the suburbs, and it all turned out badly for her* (overgeneralisation). *This is going to work out badly. It is going to be disastrous* (catastrophising). *Their decision is so disrespectful to me* (personalisation). *After all, I gave them good advice, and they just ignored it. Don't they realise how upset their decision would make me feel* (blaming)? *They should have listened to me because I have more experience than them* (shoulds). *I am right about this. She knows I am right... I have always been the sensible one. They will have to learn the hard way that they should have listened to me* (always being right).

Let's break this down and see where this person is making mistakes. This parent is obviously upset about the fact that her daughter and her daughter's husband had made a decision to sell their suburban home and move to the country.

> To start, as a basis for her objection, the parent made reference to a decision made by an aunt years ago that had a poor outcome. The parent was extrapolating the outcome from one decision to apply to all similar decisions or, at least, to those to which she disagreed. This is an example of overgeneralisation.

> The parent then predicted a terrible outcome without any real evidence that a poor outcome was likely or identifying on what they were basing their prediction. This is an example of catastrophising.

> The parent then makes the situation about them by identifying how she has interpreted the daughter's decision as a sign of disrespect. This is an example of personalisation.

> The parent then goes on to blame their upset feelings on the daughter's decision to go against their advice. This occurs despite the decision not being an unreasonable one and not being one that anyone other than the daughter and her husband should have made. This is an indication of the cognitive error of blaming.

> The parent states that the daughter should have listened to the advice they gave, even though the daughter is an adult, and the decisions made by the daughter would be in reference to her own wishes and those of her husband. This is an example of the cognitive error of shoulds.
>
> The parent concludes that they are right, and the daughter will have to suffer the consequences of going against the parent's advice. This is an example of always being right.

The errors in this person's thinking have resulted in her feeling much worse than she would have if she had not made these errors. Let's find out how to change this way of thinking to protect yourself from the negative effects of logical errors.

Understanding automatic thoughts

The goal here is to teach you to think in a more realistic and balanced way so that you can cope better and relax your need to be in control. This is done in a number of ways. Let's start this process.

Everybody experiences automatic thoughts. They reflect our way of making sense of and reacting to the world around us and to internal experiences, such as anxiety or memories and urges. Automatic thoughts are often highly believable, even when they are based on logical errors. As a result of their believability, we tend not to challenge them. If they pass unchallenged, they can have a profound and detrimental effect on our emotional state. For example, if a person thinks that a situation should have turned out some other way and they do not challenge that thought, they are likely to feel bad as a consequence.

Consider this example. This person had arranged her day, including collecting some things she wanted to borrow from her sister for a dinner party she was holding. When she tried to arrange the collection, her sister told her that she was going to be out at that time but offered some alternative times that suited the sister. Let's examine the content of this person's self-talk.

> *This won't do at all. I have arranged my day right down to the last minute. It's not fair that my sister won't be home. She should change her plans so I can drop by her place and collect the things I need. She said she would lend me the things when I asked, so she should be available when I need them.*

It would be hard to think this way without feeling angry as a consequence. We tend to believe the things we tell ourselves, even if they are not true. In this case, the sister was doing a favour, but this person thought the sister should accommodate her needs rather than the person working around her sister's availability. She was angry with her sister. It should be noted that even when we do not pay much attention to our self-talk – our running commentary – we can still be affected by it.

Catching automatic thoughts

It is important to start to pay attention to your automatic thoughts so that their content can be used to identify both the logical errors you are making and, ultimately, your core beliefs. The way to go about this is to keep a thought record related to times when you notice a change in the way you are feeling.

In its simplest form, a thought record asks you to identify the event that has occurred, to take notice of the thoughts that go through your head at the time of the event, and to record the consequences you experience, both in terms of how you feel and how you might act in response. Consider the example below of a simple thought record of a person whose family was organising a birthday celebration for their mother.

A	B	C
Activating event	Belief or thought	Consequence: emotional and behavioural
My brother and sister disagreed with me about the venue I chose for the party because they thought it cost too much.	*My brother and sister always go out of their way to disagree with me. If someone else had suggested the venue, they would have agreed.*	*I felt so frustrated I rang them both and told them they were only doing this because they hated me.*
My family disagreed with my decision to have a theme for the party.	*They are just wrong about this. I'm not giving in on this. I will show them.*	*I felt really angry. I went ahead and ordered invitations with the theme I chose.*

We do not usually pay much deliberate attention to the fact that we are having thoughts going through our heads, even though they can have such a profound effect on how we are feeling and what we choose to do as a result of feeling that way. To change our thinking, we have to learn to identify our automatic thoughts. When we consider the events that trigger a response in us, we can usually identify what went through our mind at the time.

By keeping track of your automatic thoughts, you can identify patterns in your thinking that are linked with particular negative feelings and the behaviours you choose because you are feeling that way. Use the simple thought record below to keep track of your automatic thoughts in relation to events that stress you.

Simple automatic thoughts worksheet		
A	B	C
Activating event	Belief or thought	Consequence: emotional and behavioural

Worksheet available at elemen.com.au

Understanding and noticing logical errors

Everyone makes logical errors. It is important to understand this point. It is when the error you are making (e.g., everything should be fair) conflicts with how things really are (e.g., the world is neither fair nor unfair; it just is the way it is) that problems arise. However, it is also important to be able to recognise the logical errors you are making so that you can correct them and correct the problems in your core beliefs. To start to do this, you can try the simple approach of expanding on your thought record form so that you include the types of logical errors that are reflected in your automatic thoughts.

Let's go back to our original thought record form and expand the examples.

Expanded thought record form - example			
A	B	C	D
Activating event	Belief or thought	Consequence: emotional and behavioural	Logical errors
My brother and sister disagreed with me about the venue I chose for the party because they thought it cost too much.	*My brother and sister always go out of their way to disagree with me. If someone else had suggested the venue, they would have agreed.*	*I felt so frustrated I rang them both and told them they were only doing this because they hated me.*	*Personalisation*
My family disagreed with my decision to have a theme for the party.	*They are just wrong about this. I'm not giving in on this. I will show them.*	*I felt really angry. I went ahead and ordered invitations with the theme I chose.*	*Always being right*

Despite this person's brother and sister giving a reasonable explanation for their rejection of the party venue, that is, the cost, this person has interpreted their rejection as a personal attack. In this way, this person has personalised the problem situation in a way that was unnecessary and caused them to feel frustrated. They then felt driven to escalate the problem by phoning the siblings to express this personalisation.

Against the views of all other family members, this person chose a theme for the party. This person was determined to show they were right. The anger felt in response to the rejection of the theme idea triggered a determination to prove the rightness of the idea by going ahead and ordering the invitations that, in effect, forced the issue.

Below is an expanded thought record form that you can use to identify your logical errors in what you are thinking.

Expanded thought record form			
A	B	C	D
Activating event	Belief or thought	Consequence: emotional and behavioural	Logical errors

Worksheet available at elemen.com.au

Reframing your thoughts (cognitive restructuring)

The process of challenging our negative automatic thoughts is called cognitive restructuring. This is what we are trying to achieve here. The conclusions we reach because of our logical errors should be challenged and replaced with something that is healthier and more accurately reflects how the world really works.

Although there are lots of ways you can go about restructuring your thinking, we are going to introduce you to a straightforward method. We are going to start by ensuring that you understand the difference between fact and opinion. This is important as our thoughts and decision-making should be based on facts and not the opinions we form because of incorrect information that can underlie our core beliefs. For example, an opinion would be "I am stupid". You might form this opinion because someone has repeatedly told you that you are stupid or because they acted in a way that encouraged you to believe you were stupid. It is not the truth or a fact that you are stupid. It is a belief you have or an opinion you have formed because of incorrect information.

We refer to the opinion on which you rely as a work of fiction. That is, you write a story in your head about what is happening and then act as if the story is true. You need to be able to identify when you are relying on the story you have written in your mind rather than basing your thoughts on factual evidence. Let's start by having a go at identifying fact from opinion or fiction. In the spaces provided, you can add other things you have been thinking and consider whether they are facts or opinions.

Fact or fiction worksheet		
Statement	*Fact*	*Fiction*
I am stupid		√
I love bushwalking	√	
I am ugly		
I forgot to renew my driver's licence		
No one likes me		
This will be a disaster		
I'm not good enough		
I should be able to control things		
I hate my job		
I should know what is about to happen		
There are times when people feel stressed		

Checklist available at elemen.com.au

The facts here are:

> I love bushwalking
>
> I forgot to review my driver's licence
>
> I hate my job
>
> There are times when people feel stressed

The statements that are opinions are:

> I am stupid
>
> I am ugly
>
> No one likes me
>
> This will be a disaster
>
> I'm not good enough
>
> I should be able to control things
>
> I should know what is about to happen

Why should we make this distinction between what is a fact and what is an opinion? It is because the errors in thinking we make are based on opinion and not on fact. Further, because we hold this opinion, we assume that it is true because we are thinking it and not because it is based on fact.

To tidy up our thinking and remove the logical errors, we have to rely on those thoughts that are based on fact alone. We can reject thoughts that are just based on our opinions because our opinions can be faulty. Factual information will be a good guide for us to determine whether or not we should believe what we are thinking.

Cognitive restructuring worksheet – Example
What I am thinking *My brother and sister always go out of their way to disagree with me. If someone else had suggested the venue, they would have agreed.*
Facts supporting the thought *They disagreed with my choice of venue.*
Facts contradicting the thought *The venue is really expensive, and this is the reason they rejected my idea.* *Anyone else suggesting the venue would not have changed the price of the venue.* *My brother and sister don't always disagree with me and my ideas.*
Is this thought based on factual evidence or opinion? *This thought was just based on my opinion. It really is the case that the venue is expensive which is a fact. So, my brother and sister didn't go out of their way just to disagree with me because it was my idea.*

By looking at the facts for and against a point of view being true, you can work out the value of holding that opinion. It seems like a waste of time to be thinking a particular thing and being negatively affected by it emotionally and behaviourally if you cannot even determine that the opinion reflects the truth. You can use the worksheet below to examine your thoughts in terms of the facts supporting what you are thinking and the facts that contradict what you are thinking.

Cognitive restructuring worksheet
What I am thinking
Facts supporting the thought
Facts contradicting the thought
Is this thought based on factual evidence or opinion?

Worksheet available at elemen.com.au

Making the restructured thinking habitual

To get to a point where you are thinking in a healthier way, you need to go through a process of deliberately challenging your thinking. You need to overlearn noticing your automatic thoughts and then reframe them into a healthier and more accurate alternative thought. You can then get to the point where you can challenge your thinking and adjust your automatic thoughts without giving it much attention. Eventually, you will not even have to do that because your core beliefs will be corrected to offer you a more accurate template of how the world works and how you fit into that world.

Targeting the assumptions

Let's not forget about those assumptions that underlie the errors you make in your thinking. We need to challenge those assumptions to completely correct your thinking. Remember, if the assumptions that underlie the error are shown to be wrong, there is every reason to abandon the logical error and replace it with a more logical point of view.

There are a few ways you can challenge the assumptions that underlie logical errors. We are going to focus on three approaches. Firstly, we are going to apply the strategy of looking at the advantages and disadvantages of holding an assumption. Consider the following example of someone who is predicting that things are going to work out poorly.

Assumption worksheet: Advantages and disadvantages
Logical error and assumption *Always being right. People have to choose a side, and there is a right side and a wrong side.*
Advantages *I will get my way if I try hard enough.*
Disadvantages *I will be facing a lot of conflict with people if I continue to assume I am always right.* *I will be disappointed throughout life if I am not more flexible in my thinking.* *There are lots of situations in life where there is no right and wrong side and I am going to have a difficult life if I don't accept this.*

Challenging the assumption that underlies a tendency to want to always be right, you can see that there are many more disadvantages to doing this than there are advantages. The disadvantages indicate that the holder of the assumption is facing ongoing difficulties if they continue to hold this point of view. Add other disadvantages you can think of when holding this assumption.

Secondly, you can act against the assumptions. What would happen if the assumption was incorrect? Consider the following example.

Assumption worksheet: Acting against the assumption
Logical error and assumption *Always being right. People have to choose a side, and there is a right side and a wrong side.*
Things that might happen if I acted like the assumption was not true. *I might relax instead of fighting for my point of view all the time.* *I might find that I have fewer conflicts with people.* *I might feel less of a burden of responsibility to be in charge of everything.*

By acting as if the assumption is false, you can usually identify the positive things that would occur as a consequence. All of these things are better than fighting to be right about everything. Remember, trying always to be right is stressful and exhausting. Think of other ways you could have acted against this assumption.

Finally, you can argue against the assumption. You can take the perspective that the assumption is wrong and develop an argument for your case. Consider the following example.

Assumption worksheet: Arguing against the assumption
Logical error and assumption *Always being right. People have to choose a side, and there is a right side and a wrong side.*
Arguments against the assumption *It is not possible to always be right about everything.* *People are entitled to their own opinions.* *There are lots of things in life that are a point of view, so they are not a matter of right or wrong.*

Here, you are thinking of the *facts* that can be used to present a good argument that the assumption associated with the logical error is not accurate. This will allow you to challenge your error-ridden thinking and replace it with healthier thinking that will not encourage you to feel strong, negative emotions. Can you think of other arguments you could use against the assumption?

Below is a worksheet you can use to challenge the assumptions that underlie your errors in thinking.

Targeting assumptions worksheet
Logical error and assumption
Advantages
Disadvantages
Things that might happen if I acted like the assumption was not true
Arguments against the assumption

Worksheet is available at elemen.com.au

Here, we have asked you to consider challenging the sorts of thoughts you might have that are likely to make you feel worse than you would otherwise feel if you did not think that way. You have learned to access these logical errors by paying attention to your automatic thoughts that serve as the running commentary your mind provides. You have learned ways to challenge these errors and remove them and their influence from your thinking. The goal of doing these things has been to help you manage your distress and protect yourself from distress in the future.

Recognising others' points of view

Before we move on to learning how to negotiate for what you want rather than demanding it, it is a good idea to learn how to recognise other people's points of view. People who like to be in control tend to ignore or dismiss what other people want. Alternatively, they just fail to recognise that other people's perspectives have value. This is not because they are bad people but because they are so wrapped up in their own thoughts about how they think things should happen that they fail to take the time to consider the value of alternative ways of looking at things.

So, we are going to teach you how to use empathy to take a step back from your focus on being in control by considering other people's thoughts and feelings.

What is empathy?

Empathy refers to an understanding of what another person is feeling and the reasons they are feeling that way. It is not sympathy, which is the feeling you have for someone else's suffering. In contrast, empathy is about your understanding of the other person's experience.

Empathy does not require that you agree with the other person's need to feel that way or the reason why they are feeling as they do. It does not go beyond an appreciation of the other person's experience.

What is the use of empathy?

Learning empathy skills will help you have a better appreciation of other people's perspectives. This, in turn, will help you to understand that there are points of view other than your own that have value. It will also help you understand how people are reacting to your demands to be in charge. It will also help you understand why people are choosing to reject your opinions and demands.

Learning empathy skills

We are going to get you to do some exercises that will help build up your empathy skills. Remember, you are trying to identify what the other person is feeling and why they are feeling that way. Let's consider some examples.

> *When he returned home after work, Jack's wife asked him about his day. Jack sighed and then said the following:*
>
> *"It was a long day. I had two back-to-back meetings that seemed to go on forever. There was a lot of disagreement between various people, and voices were raised. I had so much I had to do, but I had to sit through people endlessly arguing. When I finally got back to my desk, it was almost lunchtime, so I had to work through my lunch break to catch up, and I didn't get a chance to grab a breath of fresh air by going for a walk outside. My afternoon was flat out. I had a couple of things that had deadlines, so I had to rush to finish them after wasting the morning with useless meetings. I finally got them done, but it took some effort. I can tell you, I am very glad to be home."*
>
> *What is it that Jack was likely to be feeling right then when he was talking with his wife?*
>
> *Why was he feeling this way?*

In all likelihood, Jack was feeling exhausted because he had a busy day. How do we know this? We know this because Jack said so. After a frustrating morning, he worked hard for the rest of the day without a break. He said he was glad to be home.

Let's try another example. In this case, the person is feeling more than one thing. Remember, people are complex and can feel more than one thing at a time.

> *Joe and Tania recently found out that they are having their first child. They are looking forward to telling their families. However, influencing this experience is the fact that Tania's mother recently died after a long illness. Tania said the following:*
>
> *"This is such big news, and I know our families will be excited. But I wish Mum was here. I know she wanted to be a grandmother, and she would have made a wonderful grandma."*
>
> *What is Tania feeling, and why is she feeling that way?*

It seems like Tania is happy and excited about the news about their baby and wants to share the news with their families. However, she is feeling sad that her mother will not be there to share their happiness and will not be in her child's life in the future.

Let's try one more that relates to a need to exert control. Here, this person is dealing with his father's determination to exert influence over what he studies at university.

> *Michael has wanted to be a teacher for a long time. He thinks he would be good at the job, and it would be fulfilling for him. However, his father disagrees, believing he would be better off studying commerce. Michael says the following:*
>
> *"I don't know what to do. I have wanted to be a teacher for ages. I worked hard at school with the goal of going to uni to study and become a teacher. But Dad is insistent that I study commerce. He thinks I can earn more. He says he knows better than I do about what is right for me. He said he won't give me any financial support if I study teaching. My whole life is changing direction... a direction I don't want. I don't know what to do. Dad said he always gets what he wants, so I just have to get used to the idea. But this is my life. I should get to choose what path it is going to take. Despite all his past promises of support, if I went to uni, I am just going to have to manage without that support. It will be harder, but I will find a way."*
>
> *What is Michael feeling, and why is he feeling that way?*

Michael is feeling a complex range of emotions. He is upset and disappointed by his father's stance but determined to find his own way and choose his own path.

To be able to use empathy by identifying what the other person is feeling and why they are feeling that way, you need to actively listen to what the person is saying verbally or conveying in their nonverbal indicators of their emotional state. Pay attention to the other person so that you can determine the impact of what you are saying and what you are demanding of the other person. This skill will serve you well when you enter into a process to negotiate for what you want.

Assertive negotiation

When learning to manage your urge to be in control, it is not the goal that you do the opposite and always give in to other people's demands. It is important that you learn to negotiate for what you want without disregarding what the other person might want. What we are referring to here is assertive negotiation.

Assertiveness refers to standing up for your rights without trampling over the rights of others. Some people mistake assertiveness for aggressiveness, which refers to the aggressive assertion of your rights irrespective of others' rights. At the other extreme is passivity where a person will not stand up for their own rights and allow others to walk over them.

So, the aim here is to teach you to stand up for your own rights without trampling over the rights of other people. An assertive interpersonal style will allow you to negotiate for what you want without demanding that it happen.

Asking for change

Firstly, we need to consider how to assertively solve problems by making reasonable requests for change or appropriate requests for what you would like to have happen. Many people find this difficult. They will start to make a request but are easily derailed by the deflection techniques used by the other person. Alternatively, they will start to make a request but are then affected by the annoyance they feel about the response of the other person. This following step-by-step guide is designed to help you plan ahead for how you are going to manage a request for change.

Define the problem situation

You should start by defining the problem you are facing. Do this by focusing on the facts of the matter and not your interpretation of the situation. You should do this by being as specific as possible. Avoid generalisations like "It's always the case…" or "Nothing ever goes right…". Instead, keep a narrow focus on the situation you have identified that you wish to change. Limit this to one problem at a time rather than bombarding the other person with a list of grievances.

Describe how you are feeling

Here, you get a chance to describe how you feel about the situation. Remember, you are referring to how you feel and not how someone else *made* you feel. Be clear about the link between your feelings and the problem situation. Again, do not generalise to all situations or all problems.

Avoid blaming others. By blaming others, you put them on the defensive and little is ever resolved as a consequence. When you talk about how you are feeling, use what are called 'I messages'. That is, your descriptions of your feelings should start with something like "I feel…". No one can argue with you about this matter. They cannot say that you do not feel something that you have stated you feel. If you started with "You make me feel…", it is likely that the other person would argue that it was not their intention to make you feel that way, and if you do, that is your problem. Using 'I messages' allows you to avoid all of this discussion. In any case, you are the person who decides how you feel, and you should be able to relate that feeling to the other person.

This is a good opportunity to express your feelings. It is a mistake to assume that others know what you are thinking or feeling if you have not said so. If you have not said how you feel, the other person can do little more than guess. We make a mistake by assuming that someone who knows you well can 'mindread' and automatically know what you are thinking or feeling. Clear communication works much better than allowing others to guess.

Make your request for change

Here, you should make a statement about what you want to happen. You need to be brief. Do not turn your request into a lecture. Also, you need to be specific. Clearly state what you want rather than use terms that are not concrete. For example, it will not help to say, "I want things to improve" because that is a generalised statement that can be interpreted in a multitude of ways. You would be better off saying, "I want you to cook dinner two nights a week," or "I am asking you to change your work hours so that you start an hour earlier and finish an hour earlier".

Outline possible positive consequences

If the other person initially does not want to agree with your request for change, you may choose to point out the positive consequences that would follow from the agreement. Do not make wild promises. Just focus on the positive things that are likely to happen from the change you are requesting. You are building the argument for what you want. For example, you could say, "I am asking you to change your work hours so that you start an hour earlier and finish an hour earlier. If you agree, you will be able to leave before the peak hour traffic and have more time in the evenings".

Outline potential negative consequences

If the other person is still reluctant to agree with what you are asking, you can outline the likely negative consequences for them if they choose not to comply with your wishes. Do not threaten. Simply state what you understand to be the bad things that will happen if things do not change. For example, you could say, "I am asking you to change your work hours so that you start an hour earlier and finish an hour earlier. If you disagree, I will have to employ someone to start early. As I cannot just employ them for an hour, I will have to cut back your hours in the mornings so I can get someone to start at the earlier time".

It is important to remember that you should only outline negative consequences that you are certain you are willing to follow through on. You, too, have to live with the negative consequences, so do not outline something you are not willing to do or have happen.

So, to summarise, when making a request for change, do the following:

> Define the problem situation
>
> Describe how you are feeling
>
> Make your request for change
>
> Outline possible positive consequences
>
> Outline potential negative consequences

This is a good approach to standing up for your rights in an assertive manner. It is relatively simple and straightforward. You can also work out in advance what it is you want to say and this protects you from having to make it up on the spot.

However, standing up for your rights may not be enough in itself if you are aiming for assertive communication. You need to be able to negotiate for what you want with a person who may be inclined not to give this to you. Consider the following negotiation process.

Negotiating for what you want

To negotiate with another person, your starting point needs to be that you both have needs that are equally important. This will require some effort on your part. It is easy for us to assume that what we want is right and what the other person wants is wrong. However, if you hold this view, then any interaction about the issue in question will be an argument rather than a negotiation.

There are six steps that should be taken when you enter into a negotiation. Let's consider each of these steps.

Know what it is you want

Know what it is that you are negotiating for. You must have a clearly defined goal if you are to enter into a negotiation. If you are not clear about what you want, then how can the other person have any idea?

Make a statement of what you want in specific terms

In specific terms and being as clear as possible, make a statement about what you want or do not want to have happen. This can be in terms of what you want or do not want the other person to do. However, it may also be in terms of what you want as the outcome.

Listen to the point of view of the other person

Your goal here is to understand the other person's perspective. To do this, you have to listen carefully to what the other person has to say about their point of view. You should use active listening skills where you can ask for clarification or elaboration. Remember, you may not agree with the other person's perspective. What you should be doing is appreciating that they have a point of view that might be different from yours, but it is their point of view nonetheless.

Make a proposal

Next, you should make a proposal that offers a resolution. The proposal should not be solely based on what you want. It should take into account the other person's needs. This can be a challenging step that may take some thought on your part. It is easier to conceptualise a proposal that takes into account what both of you want if you approach it with the goal of achieving a 'win-win' outcome. This is where you get some of what you want, and the other person gets some of what they want. A win-win proposal has a much better chance of being accepted than a 'my way or the highway' approach.

Ask for a counterproposal

If your proposal is not accepted, do not be disheartened. Ask the other person for a counterproposal. Remember that your goal is to reach a point where you can both accept the proposal, even if you both do not get all of what you want.

Aim for compromise

The end result of any negotiation is typically a compromise. You are unlikely to get everything your way, but neither is the other person. You are aiming to reach a middle point that is satisfactory to you both. There are a variety of ways a compromise can be achieved:

> You give up some of what you want to gain some of what you want, and so does the other person.

> You might split the difference.

> You might agree that you do it your way when you are in control, and the other person does it their way when they are in control.

Remember, the goal here is to negotiate for what you want rather than demand. A negotiated agreement may call for compromise but should be positive for both you and the other person in some ways.

Some final thoughts

There are a few points that need to be stated or re-stated.

> Your need to feel in control feels right and makes sense to you. From your perspective, your belief that you know the right way of doing things feels sensible and normal. However, your need to be in control is causing you to disregard the views of others, and others can resent this.
>
> However, being right and others being wrong is not really the issue. It is more the case that there are a multitude of perspectives about any one issue and lots of ways of approaching any task. If you ignore the perspectives of others, you close yourself off to a broader and more flexible approach to life.
>
> Although it feels like you could never give up the need to be in control, it is possible if you approach things in the right way. Learn the strategies we have suggested to make this easier for you. But it is also about adopting the right attitude. Rather than seeing this as you giving something up, see any change you make as a broadening of your experience and an increase in your wisdom. In this way, by learning to do things differently, you are gaining something.

We wish you well with your efforts to change.

Additional readings

Kennerley, H., Kirk, J., & Westbrook, D. (2016). *An introduction to cognitive behaviour therapy: Skills and applications (3rd edn.).* London: Sage Publications.

Paterson, R.J. (2023). *The assertiveness workbook: How to express your ideas and stand up for yourself at work and in relationships.* London: New Harbinger Publications.

www.ingramcontent.com/pod-product-compliance
Lightning Source LLC
Chambersburg PA
CBHW080856090426
42735CB00014B/3170